GOD WINK

CHRISTMAS

STORIES

READ ABOUT MORE AMAZING
GODWINKS IN THESE BOOKS:

When God Winks

God Winks on Love

Godwink Stories

Godwinks and Divine Alignment

The Godwink Effect

The 40 Day Prayer Challenge

GOD WINK

CHRISTMAS

STORIES

✻

Discover the Most Wondrous Gifts of the Season

SQuire Rushnell
and Louise DuArt

ILLUSTRATIONS BY GAIL FOERSTER

Includes previously published stories from
Godwink series books and *The 40 Day Prayer Challenge*

HOWARD BOOKS
—
ATRIA

New York   London   Toronto   Sydney   New Delhi

An Imprint of Simon & Schuster, Inc.
1230 Avenue of the Americas
New York, NY 10020

First Howard Books / Atria Books paperback edition October 2019

HOWARD BOOKS / **ATRIA** BOOKS and colophon are trademarks of Simon & Schuster, Inc.

For information about special discounts for bulk purchases,
please contact Simon & Schuster Special Sales at 1-866-506-1949
or business@simonandschuster.com.

The Simon & Schuster Speakers Bureau can bring authors
to your live event. For more information or to book an event,
contact the Simon & Schuster Speakers Bureau at 1-866-248-3049
or visit our website at www.simonspeakers.com.

Interior design by Silverglass
Illustrations by Gail Foerster

Page 117: photo at left courtesy of Dan Cummins; image at right is in the public domain.

Manufactured in the United States of America

10 9 8 7 6 5 4 3 2

Library of Congress Cataloging-in-Publication Data is available.

ISBN 978-1-5011-9995-0
ISBN 978-1-5011-9996-7 (pbk)
ISBN 978-1-5011-9997-4 (ebook)

CONTENTS

INTRODUCTION

Imagine that you have just opened the door to this book. And you are awaiting wondrous gifts that will enrich your life!

With the joy you once felt as a child, arising with wide-eyed delight on Christmas morning, every Godwink story on the following pages is a beautifully wrapped gift, just for you.

Think of it. Out of seven billion people on the planet, a Godwink is a direct, person-to-person message of hope and encouragement.

We believe that as the following true-life stories unfold they will trigger memories of your own Godwinks, extraordinary things that have happened to you; things you perhaps wondered about and maybe even dismissed as too unbelievable to believe.

Now you can believe them. This book proves that God-winks happen to everyone. They are universal—crossing every border, every religion—because, as the ancient scriptures tell us,[1] a tiny bit of faith the size of a mustard seed is all you need to begin developing your vision to see your Godwinks. And once you see them, the more you'll see them, all around you, every day.

As you are drawn into the lives of the people who lived the thirty amazing stories in this book, you'll imagine you're alongside them as their Godwinks are revealed, as if you were in the middle of a minimovie with a surprise ending.

You'll sense you're with Sandy, a beleaguered pre-Christmas mother, rushing through a supermarket, as she realizes the joy of an incredible gift of kindness. You'll be in a children's hospital at Christmas with the actress Roma Downey as she opens her gift of purpose—her job for God. You'll take a romantic journey with Brooke, who's uncertain that she'll ever find Prince Charming, and you'll be next to her as she discovers the gift of reassurance that's awaiting her, like a scene from *It's a Wonderful Life*.

Looking on expectantly and lovingly is the Giver of every good gift; your Creator, who personally wrapped your presents and put them under the tree. He's saying, "Go ahead . . . open them! They may change your life forever!"

—*SQuire and Louise*

The new word, now appearing in dictionaries:

G

God-wink (n.)
A "coincidence" that is not coincidence but instead originates from a divine source.

Another term for "answered prayer."

Note: Most of the stories in this book are brand-new. A few are "classics," previously published, now rewritten and updated. The latter are marked with this symbol:

1

Sandy: Godwinks
and Giftwinks

Like so many women on Christmas Eve, Sandy Locke had a lot to get done. She moves like a Road Runner cartoon, in a figurative cloud of dust, zooming from store to store—*beep beep*—checking and rechecking her lists—*beep beep*—watching the clock like a coach in the final seconds of a game.

Sandy and Rick Locke's daughter had invited them for Christmas Eve, with a request for Sandy to bring one of her special dishes: her delicious gluten-free Strawberry Jell-O Pretzel Salad. Two of the family members were gluten intolerant.

Rapidly, Sandy and Rick pushed their cart through the supermarket, grabbing things they needed—and too many more they didn't—trying to get to the checkout as fast as possible.

Darn. The store didn't carry the *one* item Sandy absolutely had to have for her special salad: gluten-free pretzels.

She looked at Rick. "Why don't I drop you at home? You put away the groceries, and I'll run over to Albertson's to see if they have 'em."

Rick nodded.

"Tell you what," she continued as an afterthought, "while I'm checking out, why don't you bring the car up. I'll meet you out front."

Rick again nodded and disappeared.

Sandy lunged her cart forward, then immediately was slowed. Blocking the aisle was an older couple. Sandy looked to see if she could squeeze by. No. Not possible. They were moving very deliberately, both holding on to the cart to steady themselves.

Other customers began to display annoyance, rolling their eyes, heaving sighs. But as Sandy looked at them, something caught a piece of her heart, a tenderness that was evident between the two of them.

When the opportunity arose, she circled into another aisle, found an available checkout, and soon saw Rick waiting in their car out front.

A short while later, they pulled into their driveway. As Rick gathered up the groceries, Sandy slid into the driver's seat and said, "I'll try not to be too long."

At Albertson's, Sandy didn't bother with a cart or basket but headed directly to the gluten-free area. *Thank goodness, there they are!* she thought as she grabbed what she needed.

As she headed for the shortest checkout line, she saw a few other things and, on impulse, piled them onto her now overloaded arms.

The line wasn't moving; then she saw why.

Two places ahead in the line was the older couple she had seen from the other store. They were methodically counting out their money to pay the bill. Sandy watched as the lady took out what appeared to be a gift stamp book, looking at the cashier with anticipation.

The customer standing between Sandy and the older couple was now making smacking sounds and groans.

Sandy looked above the register. A sign described an Albertson's holiday promotion. For every ten-dollar purchase you would receive a single stamp toward gift items, silverware, etc.

The cashier handed the older woman her stamps, and, as her husband watched, she began to paste them into her book.

The cashier, sensing the growing anxiety of the next customer, asked the older couple if they would mind stepping to the side to finish their task.

Sandy's eyes followed as the sweet couple shuffled off a short distance and stopped to glue their stamps into the book. She saw simultaneous disappointment descend upon their faces. Their already slumped shoulders seemed to sag further. They must have been saving up for something they needed and didn't have enough stamps.

The older man put his arm on his wife's shoulders, comforting her.

Sandy's arms were getting weary with all the items she was carrying. And now the impatient person ahead of her was challenging the price of something. A courtesy clerk was called to go check a price.

Everyone waited.

Just as the courtesy clerk returned, Sandy strained to see where the older couple was. She saw the dejected pair shuffling behind their cart, exiting the store.

There was an unmistakable sense of dearness between the man and woman. He helped her, and she helped him.

Feeling helpless, she whispered a prayer, just "Please Lord . . . bless them."

It dawned on her that in a single moment, with a sweet snapshot, she had been lifted from all of the anxiety—the pressure to get everything done, the hassles in the check-out line—and that God had provided her with a peace that surpassed all understanding.

"Next."

It was the cashier, pulling her attention back to the matters at hand.

Sandy was surprised that her total came to a little over forty dollars. It occurred to her that if she had purchased only what she had come in for, it would have been around five.

Now the cashier was handing her change and four stamps.

She looked at them. She knew what she had to do: find that older couple!

Now she had a new anxiety. Could she find those dear people in that big parking lot? Several minutes had already passed since they'd left the store.

Running was no longer an option for Sandy's knees, but she rushed as quickly as she could. She scanned the handicapped parking areas.

There they were!

The wife was just getting into the driver's seat. Her husband was already in the passenger seat.

Not wanting to frighten her, Sandy walked briskly, speaking loudly, saying, "Excuse me. I noticed you're collecting stamps. Would you like mine?"

She held out the four stamps.

The lady's mouth opened slightly. Her eyes filled with tears. And she reached for her stamp collection book.

"Oh. Oh, my goodness. We've been saving stamps for a Christmas gift for our daughter. Silverware." The lady held up the book to show Sandy the empty spaces for stamps. "You're not going to believe this. We just needed four more stamps!" She smiled at Sandy with childlike wonder. "Thank you so very much," she said with twinkling eyes.

Sandy returned the smile. "Merry Christmas," she said with a lump in her throat.

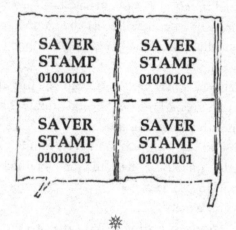

❄

The lane to exit Albertson's parking lot routed traffic past the front of the store. Sandy had to bring her car to a stop. The older couple was now shuffling past the front of her car, returning to redeem their stamps and get their daughter's gift.

Tears came to Sandy's eyes. God's fingerprints were all over every detail of that day, leaving her with one of her favorite God memories.

"Thank you, God," said Sandy, realizing she'd just been given the stamp of approval . . . to be a Godwink Link—the unexpected deliverer of a Christmas Godwink to someone else!

REFLECTIONS

You, like Sandy, have probably found yourself barreling toward a destination when all of a sudden God prompts you to make a U-turn. You find yourself at a crossroads where you need to make a choice.

You ask yourself: Should I stop in my tracks, turn around, and tend to the needs of someone else? Or should I continue on with my intended mission?

Sandy was up against the clock, feeling there wasn't enough time in the day to complete everything on her to-do list. The fact is, it doesn't matter if you're rich or poor, famous or unknown, God has given each of us 1,440 minutes in a day. The question is, what are you going to do with your gift of time?

In Sandy's case, when opportunity knocked, she made the choice to slow down and allow God to work through her. To her it seemed like such a small gesture, but she soon found out that the smallest package often contains the most precious gift. Such as the gift of kindness.

Each of you should use whatever gift you have received
to serve others, as faithful stewards
of God's grace in its various forms.
—1 Peter 4:10 (NIV)

2

Jonna: The Extraordinary Gift

You'd never have known she was painfully shy.

Nine-year-old Jonna Fitzgerald spent hours gliding across the front porch, her stage, smiling demurely and waving to legions of fans.

Jonna's princess tiara, cut from a margarine tub, glued and sparkled, perched atop her long auburn hair. Makeup, a bit too rosy on her cheeks, matched the long train of her make-believe gown rescued from sheets swiped from the laundry bin.

Jonna was emulating her heroine, Miss Texas 1973, Judy Mallett. She had been captivated from the moment she'd seen Judy in a whirlwind of fiddle playing during the televised talent competition. She had instantly resolved: she, too, wanted to learn to play the fiddle so she could be just like Miss Texas.

That September, when school started, Jonna got her first Godwink.

She brought home a flyer that had been handed out by

the music teacher. It said that a new program was going to begin, called Mini Strings. A violin teacher would be coming to the school two mornings a week to teach students who were interested.

Jonna couldn't wait to tell her mother that she wanted to sign up. She knew in her heart that if she wanted to be Miss Texas when she grew up, she would have to learn to play the fiddle like Judy Mallett.

Conversely, Mrs. Fitzgerald couldn't wait to surprise her daughter; she'd read in the paper that the fiddle-playing Judy Mallett was going to be appearing just a couple hours' drive from their home in Tyler. And she'd gotten tickets!

✳

Jonna could hardly contain her excitement when the big day arrived. On the drive, all the way there, Mrs. Fitzgerald heard every morsel of information her daughter had ever gleaned about Judy Mallett: how she did her hair, how long she practiced her fiddle, her favorite ice cream flavor . . . this, that, everything.

When they arrived at the venue, people were lined up outside. Eventually they got to their seats, and the performance began. Jonna must have told her mom a dozen times that she thought the next song was going to be her favorite, "Orange Blossom Special."

But Judy Mallett saved the best for last!

Even better, at the end of the performance Judy said she would be signing autographs and that she'd be giving away signed copies of her 45 rpm hit, "Orange Blossom Special."

Jonna looked at her mom. Her mouth dropped with excitement!

Quickly they joined the crowd that moved toward the stage as Judy's helpers yelled out instructions for everyone to get into line. Uncharacteristically for a shy child, Jonna was determined to meet her idol. As she got closer, she watched how Judy would pull a record from a bag, sign it, and hand it to the next person in line.

Her heart was beating faster as it became her turn. She had worried that she might be too shy to say anything. But she blurted out, "I'm learning to play the fiddle, and I want to be Miss Texas, just like you!" Her own courage startled her.

Judy nodded quickly, smiled, and looked at Jonna with deep sincerity. "If you practice hard, every day, and say your prayers, your dreams can come true," she said. She reached into her bag, but suddenly a look of sadness came over her face. "Oh, I'm so sorry, my dear. I've just given out my last record." She shook her head. "I don't have any more."

Jonna was crestfallen. She hadn't even imagined such a possibility. She tried to hide her disappointment—and to hold back the tears that were straining to burst out.

"But, I do have something for you, an autographed photo," she said sweetly, handing it to Jonna—while looking past her, indicating that the next person should step forward.

On the drive home Jonna was quiet. Her mother knew she was upset. She tried to cheer her up. "Honey, let's count our blessings, shall we? Miss Texas herself gave you a priceless treasure that she was saving especially for you. She gave you the gift of encouragement. She told you that if you practice every day, you too can one day be Miss Texas."

Jonna allowed her mother's kind perspective to sink in. After they got home, Judy Mallett's autographed picture found a prominent place on Jonna's bedroom wall.

And she took her heroine's encouragement to heart. She practiced and practiced.

❋

Twelve years later, in July, Jonna made it into the finals of the Miss Texas competition! Her talent performance won rave reviews. With dizzying speed she played "Orange Blossom Special," and the commentators could hardly contain their enthusiasm. When she was crowned Miss Texas 1985, the headline writers couldn't help themselves, proclaiming "Lone Star State Gets Its Second Fiddle-Playing Miss Texas."

Jonna knew that her Miss Texas demands for personal appearances would require her to crisscross America's second-largest state from end to end, over and over. Yet because her reign coincided with the Texas Sesquicentennial, her calendar began to fill up rapidly—even one date five months in advance, a bank owner booking her for his annual employee Christmas party in December.

She rapidly learned that a year as Miss Texas was going to be the next best thing to getting a PhD in human relations. Living out of a suitcase, she'd often make appearances in three or four cities in a single day, losing track of where she was. She had no idea that she was on her way to earning the dubious award for making more appearances than any prior titleholder in pageant history.

She met hundreds of people and encountered every situation. Most were pleasant, but some were scary and highly challenging for a young single woman from a small city in east Texas. Jonna was both shocked and disillusioned to discover that her lifelong dream had a dark side. In later newspaper accounts, she and other young women shared stories of unsavory advances that had been made toward them.

As December approached, Jonna felt emotionally wounded and road weary. Her princess tiara was lacking the luster she had imagined as a little girl on her front porch in Tyler. Her prayers increasingly took the form of a plea: *God, why is this so difficult? What am I supposed to learn from this turmoil? Please help me understand.*

When she finally arrived at the bank Christmas party booked long before, the wife of the bank owner met Jonna with a warm but sad greeting. She told her that her husband had passed away just a couple of weeks before. But he had been adamant that the celebration for his employees be held just as it was every year.

After Jonna's performance, which electrified her audience with her charm and extraordinary fiddle playing, the widow of the bank owner stepped to the microphone to give out gifts of recognition to the employees. She surprised Jonna by calling her back to the stage. "My dear husband was looking forward to meeting you," she said, "and before he died, he personally wrapped a gift for you." Choking back tears, she smiled slightly, and said, "He asked me to be certain that Miss Texas receive this package. He didn't tell me what was in it, just that 'it's something she needs.'"

Jonna was puzzled as to what could be inside the small, beautifully wrapped package. As a hundred or so employees looked on, she carefully opened it. Her astonishment was incalculable! Inside the box was a 45 rpm record of "Orange Blossom Special"! It had been autographed by Judy Mallett, Miss Texas 1973!

God had used a man she'd never met, who had known almost nothing about her—and surely nothing about her disappointment at the age of nine—to send her a Godwink that profoundly changed her life.

By clearing up a childhood disappointment through a remarkable gift from a stranger, whom she will meet only in the *next* lifetime, God let her know that He had placed her exactly where He had planned for her to be; that she had been doing His work, and He was pleased.

Jonna represented Texas in the 1986 Miss America pageant, winning second runner-up. She received a rare standing ovation for her rousing fiddle performance of "Orange Blossom Special." Today she is the district director for Congressman Louie Gohmert of Texas.

REFLECTIONS

The disappointment of a little girl was buried deeply in Jonna's heart. She really wanted that "Orange Blossom Special" 45 rpm from her Miss Texas hero.

Over the years, that disappointment faded into a distant memory. But God never forgot. He knew that the gift she had hoped to receive as a young girl would have a much more powerful meaning for her at a later time and place.

That time was after Jonna had traveled down countless roads and had begun to feel disillusioned and weary. She questioned her purpose—what was it all for? What was she supposed to learn?

> *Who knows but that you*
> *have come to your royal position*
> *for such a time as this?*
> —ESTHER 4:14 (NIV)

Yet as soon as Jonna opened that special gift, she knew exactly what she had learned: that God's magnificent gift of grace was guiding her every step along her path.

> *A gift opens the way*
> *and ushers the giver*
> *into the presence of the great.*
> —PROVERBS 18:16 (NIV)

We live life forward but so often understand it backward. You cannot see all that God has planned for you. But you can trust that He holds your future in His hands and that He has a plan to guide your steps and light your path.

Trust in the LORD *with all your heart,*
and lean not on your own understanding;
in all your ways acknowledge Him,
and He shall direct your paths.

—PROVERBS 3:5–6 (NKJV)

Whenever you think God has forgotten about you, remember Jonna's story. He didn't forget the desires in the heart of that little girl. He won't forget yours, either.

3

Carla: A Lost Christmas—Found

"My marriage is a wreck!" cried Carla.

It didn't seem possible that the images of a blissful life together that she had imagined on her wedding day, only three years earlier, were now crashing upon the shoals of life, hopelessly broken.

Separating from her husband seemed like the only reasonable option for her. It was terrible timing with Christmas only a few days away, but she had no choice. She was desperate. What would she do? Where could she go?

She couldn't bear the thought of telling her family what was going on. It was still too painful. The last thing she wanted was to face a flurry of family questions that she couldn't answer or to provide explanations she didn't have.

One of Carla's coworkers, Sally, reached out to her and offered her a place to live while she sorted things out. Carla was very grateful. Yet it seemed strange, leaving the house that she and her husband had fixed up to perfection and moving into someone else's home, sleeping in a twin bed in a tiny, low-ceilinged attic room.

She remained torn. Should she call her family? No. Every time she thought about it she concluded that it just wasn't the right time. Not Christmastime.

Sally could feel her friend's heartache. She could see it in her face, hear it in her voice. She invited Carla to her mother's house, to spend Christmas Eve with her family.

Carla declined, saying she would prefer to stay in her attic room by herself. Trying to make a joke of it, she told Sally, "I'm very grateful for your offer, but I want to spend Christmas Eve wallowing in self-pity, bingeing on old movies and eating cold pizza." What she really meant was "I have nothing to celebrate. I feel lost, confused, and alone."

❄

On Christmas Eve, Carla said good-bye to Sally, wished her "Merry Christmas," and then went up to her room. She wondered if God was watching. Curled up on the twin bed, she prayed, asking Him for a sign that things would work out.

At 8:30 p.m. the phone rang. It was Sally, imploring her to change her mind, to come spend the evening with her family. She said that they had all decided it wasn't right for Carla to be alone on Christmas and everyone was urging her to come over. "It's only a thirty-minute drive," insisted Sally. "Come on. It'll be good for you."

Trying to resist, Carla kept clinging to her private pity

party, even though it wasn't much of a party. Then she surprised herself upon hearing another part of her, saying almost involuntarily, "Oh, okay."

❋

It was cold, windy, and snowing as she scraped the windshield, just enough to see through it, and slipped into the car. Squinting, hugging the wheel, the road barely visible ahead of her, Carla kept punishing herself for being weak and succumbing to Sally's coaxing.

It was nearly 9:30 by the time Carla found Sally's mom's house and made her way to the front door. As she walked into the house, she felt more depressed than ever. There was a family of brothers, sisters, cousins, aunts, and uncles all having a great time celebrating together. She thought, *They are all strangers to me. I'm the proverbial fifth wheel.*

Carla couldn't believe it when Sally handed her a warm plate. "Mom saved you something. She thought you needed a home-cooked meal," said Sally with a smile. Fact was, Carla was hungry. And the food tasted good.

As the evening wore on, Carla began to warm up, open up, and go with the flow. Pretty soon she was laughing and enjoying being with everyone in the family.

❋

At one point, one of the uncles announced that he had checked the weather conditions and all the roads were closed.

Those who had been planning on going home for the night would have no choice but to hunker down and stay. That brought on a flurry of chatter, some voicing disappointment, others joking that it would save them a trip back the next day.

Sally and her mother handed Carla a sleeping bag and pointed to a spot on the living room floor. As she tucked in for the night, she felt out of sorts all over again. *What am I doing here with strangers, on Christmas Eve, sleeping on the floor?* she wondered. Eventually she gave in to her emotional exhaustion and drifted off to sleep.

❋

Noises in the kitchen caused her to stir and realize that Christmas morning had arrived. She wasn't ready to get up and greet anyone cheerily. Pulling the sleeping bag up a bit more, she pretended to remain asleep.

Now what should I do? she wondered. She entered into a state of dread, imagining the family running around gaily opening presents while "Miss Fifth Wheel" huddled in a corner, trying to make herself inconspicuous.

Squinting through one eye, she could see that there was now a lot of movement in the living room . . . people in PJs, some borrowed, were gathering around the tree, becoming more vocal and excited.

How long can I stay in this sleeping bag? she wondered. Now she could hear them calling out names and distributing presents.

God, let me vanish, please!

"Carla!"

What? Why are they calling me?

"Carla, here's a present for you."

How can that be? she thought as she opened her eyes and sat up.

Someone came toward her, handing her a present wrapped in red tissue paper. Someone's name had been crossed out, and "Carla" had been written in. She was stunned and speechless. But before she could finish opening her gift, her name was called again. "Carla. Another one for you."

Someone else delivered Carla's second gift. This one was wrapped in colorful gold-and-green-striped paper with a red ribbon. Again, the tag had someone's name scratched out, and written in ink was "Carla."

And so it went.

Carla realized that this group of strangers had each taken one of their gifts and put her name on it so she would be welcomed into their family and have something to open on Christmas morning.

"I can't tell you the feeling of warmth, love, and acceptance I felt at that moment," said Carla when she reflected on that day. "This was by far the closest I felt to the true meaning of Christmas that I had ever known."

She remembered that she had prayed for a sign. "That morning, with those people, I saw the human manifestation of God's Love. I was meant to be there to experience it. That was my sign—a Godwink—attesting that no matter how low you feel or what troubles you may have, God is always there. Right there next to you."

REFLECTIONS

We all feel sorry for ourselves now and again, but let's face it, a pity party isn't fun. The likely guests are bitterness, hopelessness, and depression. Carla was entertaining all three!

Even though she had been given an invitation to be with Sally's family for Christmas, she didn't feel comfortable. Her situation was like that song from *Sesame Street*:

> One of these things is not like the others.
> One of these things just doesn't belong.[1]

She was wondering where she belonged.

Like Carla, you may have wondered, *Does God see me?* He always does. You *matter* to Him and are never forgotten. That means you are never alone.

Carla learned the true meaning of Christmas. It's about giving to others and not expecting anything in return.

When you give the gift of sharing, as Sally's family did, it can last a lifetime. And for Carla, it became the most unforgettable Christmas ever!

4

SQuire: The Birth of Godwinks on Christmas Eve

This story is about Godwinks: how the word was birthed and how it has entered into our language and dictionaries.

It started on Christmas Eve with a Godwink linked to my hero, subsequently involving me—in an extraordinary manner—and in due course, resulting in the first Godwinks book finding its way onto Oprah Winfrey's nightstand.

Follow that?

Hopefully, by the end of this story, you'll see that this is really a journey about all of us: how God is using you, me, my wife, Louise, and many other Godwinkers to help spread the word "Godwink" into culture, providing people with a new way to explain how God communicates with each of us, at all times, through all things, to bring us hope and encouragement.

Once upon a time there was a picture-postcard church called Quaker Hill Church, overlooking a pastoral view of rolling mountains in upstate New York. Its traditional white steeple and small-paned windows brought to mind a Grandma Moses painting.

How I even ended up at this little church, well off the beaten path, is totally divine alignment. You see, after attending, I discovered that Quaker Hill Church was located directly across the road from the country home of my boyhood hero, Dr. Norman Vincent Peale, the author of *The Power of Positive Thinking.*

That book had a profound impact on my life. In fact, I can say that Dr. Peale's speaking style and philosophy had more influence upon me during my coming-of-age years than any other.

After that I became a member of Quaker Hill Church and had the honor to get to know Dr. and Mrs. Peale, who were occasionally in attendance and always gracious. They became sweet, dear friends.

On five occasions, when the pastor was away, I was invited to speak from the pulpit on Sunday morning. You can imagine my thrill when sometimes I looked out and saw that Dr. Peale, a man I sought to emulate, was sitting in his regular pew and, as far as I could tell, had not once nodded off to sleep!

For my sixth talk I was scheduled, months in advance, to speak in early January. I chose a topic that had always fascinated me: "Coincidence: Is It Evidence of God's Grand Plan?"

❋

On Christmas morning, days before my speech, the members of our church were notified that our prominent and beloved neighbor Dr. Peale had slipped from his earthly residence the night before and been taken, on the wings of angels, to his new heavenly home. He had died on Christmas Eve and would be laid to rest behind our church.

I couldn't help but feel that it was an incredible "coincidence" in and of itself that Dr. Peale would pass from Earth to Heaven on that very day.

I referenced that observation in the opening re-
marks of my talk. "The President of the United States
recently said something that resonated with each of
us about Dr. Norman Vincent Peale. He said, 'What a
coincidence that Dr. Peale, who devoted his entire life
to the celebration of Jesus Christ, should be called to
God's side on the very eve that the world celebrates the
birth of Christ.' "

I paused and looked directly at my audience. "What
do you think? Was that 'coincidence'? I wonder."

※

Well, that started it. What now is known as the Godwinks
Thesis was born in that moment, on that day in 1993, in
front of those people, in that little church.

During the next thirty minutes I told several incredible stories of coincidence that I had encountered over
the years and realized that I was connecting with my
audience as at no previous time. I was looking at adults
who had the facial animation of children listening to an
astonishing bedtime story. Their body language encouraged me with smiles, nods, and wide-eyed wonder. After
that day various members of the congregation urged me
to write a book on the topic.

Soon I began to understand the cold, hard lesson of
becoming an author: that it's a long process.

- Three years was how long it took me to develop the discipline to put my fingers on the keys every single day—in my case, from 5 to 7 a.m., prior to starting my day job.
- One year was how long it took to find a literary agent who believed in my book, and to help present it to publishers.
- Almost an additional year was spent figuring out what to call a "coincidence" once I concluded that many people believe that there *is* no such thing as coincidence.

That last point demands an explanation. For months Louise and I wrestled with the challenge of finding just the right word to describe a "coincidence that isn't." We discovered that in Hebrew there is no word for "coincidence." If everything comes from God, coincidence doesn't exist. I knew that faith was somehow involved, and one day the word "Godwink" just floated into my mind. I thought, *Hmmm, that sounds friendly . . . like godsend or Godspeed.* I took out my manuscript and replaced every use of the word "coincidence" with "Godwink." It fit!

Soon people were adopting the word into their own conversations, easily filling a vacancy in the language. One pastor in Las Vegas said, "'Godwink' is a friendly, nonthreatening way to describe something we've always believed about God's communications to us, but we just didn't know what to call it."

✻

Getting a publisher to gamble on an unknown author was a humbling experience. I had proudly told every publishing executive that I had been in charge of ABC's *Good Morning America* the first time the show went number one.

After thirty turndowns, I realized that my *GMA* history had impressed *me* a lot more than it did them.

My thirty-first pitch was to a small publisher in Portland, Beyond Words Publishing. The people there liked the concept of Godwinks and, for a low advance, decided to take a chance on the original book, *When God Winks*.

That brought me to another awakening: even though I'd been writing and pitching for about eight years, I had arrived only at the beginning.

Yes, that's what I said.

One veteran author described the process this way: "My publisher's job is to get the book on the shelf. My job is to get it off!"

In that clear, cold assessment, I realized that no matter how hard you think you worked to write the book, your hardest job is just about to begin.

Moreover, as excited as you think your publisher is about your baby, it is in fact just one more book on the company's big plate.

At Barnes & Noble, where about 200,000 books sit on the shelves, you're just one more pack of paper.[1]

So how does one little book scramble to the top and get attention over all the rest?

Publicity, of course!

And one soon concludes that there's an unspoken expectation that you, the author, will be generating most of that publicity. The publisher will do the best it can, usually assigning a PR person for about three months, but then you're generally expected to be on your own. You need to hire your own PR representative and/or make your own relentless calls to the media.

I now understand why famous people who are not necessarily great writers are more readily published than great writers who are not famous: they can get on TV to promote their books.

※

All right, enough whining about the woes of an author! Because, as Louise will tell you, I've loved every second of this journey!

Let's get to the big question on the mind of every author during those days. How in the world do you get booked on *The Oprah Winfrey Show*?

During the first year that *When God Winks* was in the marketplace, I hired four different PR people to make pitches to *Oprah Winfrey Show* producers, most without a peep in return. But what a thrill it was the day a lady named Alice McGee called, said she was Oprah's book booker, and told me the most enchanting words any author can hear:

"I love your book. Oprah will love your book!"

My heart soared.

One week later came the tragedy of 9/11. All shows for the entire season—on *Oprah* and every other talk show—were revamped to deal with a nation in mourning. Unfortunately, no one in the mainstream media saw any merit in a segment about the inspirational stories found in my little book.

I did receive extraordinary support from *The 700 Club* on the ABC Family Channel and a considerable number of radio programs, but national television turned a deaf ear. People who had worked with me when I had run *Good Morning America* were now working at talk shows throughout the medium, yet the answer to my PR people was pretty much the same: "Tell SQuire we love him. We hate the title of his book."

Yes, that three-letter word, G-O-D, was the impediment for many talk show bookers. Ironically, among the public, it was the title that many people gave as the reason for being drawn to the book in the first place.

Then a major Godwink occurred.

I was scheduled to appear on *Hour of Power* at the Crystal Cathedral in Anaheim, California, on Mother's Day,

2003. I told my publisher that that powerful TV ministry was available to be viewed in more than 300 million homes every Sunday morning.

"You better get a lot more books in the pipeline," I enthusiastically counseled my publisher, Richard Cohn, ever certain that his company's supply was falling short of the demand I would be whipping up.

"I think we can afford to put five thousand books in the system," said Richard, consulting the company financials.

"What? That's not enough," I complained.

That's when I realized the downside to being published by a small publisher.

Though I was elated with Beyond Words' creativity, design, and editorial sense and loved the friendly accessibility to publisher Richard Cohn, a publishing company's ability to quickly put significant numbers of books into the pipeline is dictated by the strength of its cash flow. After 9/11, through no fault of their own, many of Beyond Words' vendors were late in their payments or simply walking away from their bills.

Truth be known, my publisher was struggling to keep the doors open.

Looking skyward, I prayerfully asked, "What am I going to do, Lord? I finally get international TV exposure on *Hour of Power*, and there aren't going to be enough books in the stores."

My hopes were crashing.

But my wonderful wife, Louise, had an idea. "We can't let this opportunity pass," she said. "If our publisher can't afford it, let's put $20,000 worth of books on our credit card."

Gulp!

That was my gulp.

The second gulp came from my publisher, who, I don't believe, had ever received an offer like that. But when *Hour of Power* went on the air on Mother's Day and *When God Winks* shot to number twenty-one on Amazon, there were indeed enough books in the stores. And the publisher paid us back for the loan, right on time.

❀

What we didn't know was that our faith in the book would open the way for another extraordinary Godwink to unfold a few weeks later.

Judith Curr, the president of a new Simon & Schuster imprint, Atria Books, was making the annual pilgrimage that all publishers make to Ann Arbor, Michigan, the headquarters of Borders and Waldenbooks. At the conclusion of Judith's presentation about her new fall catalog, a young buyer of inspirational books named Marcella Clashman approached her and said the most perfect words for the ears of a publisher.

"The book you really ought to get is *When God Winks*—we can't keep it on the shelf." She had observed the increased sales of our book every time there was media attention, particularly after the *Hour of Power* broadcast.

"What's it about?" asked Judith.

"The power of coincidence in our lives," replied Marcella.

Judith was very attentive. Marcella had no way of knowing that a few years before, in Australia, Judith Curr had become a star in publishing circles by launching an unknown book called *The Celestine Prophecy*, which was all about coincidence.

Marcella's perfect words, striking the perfect ears, were an incredible Godwink.

That was on a Friday. The following Monday, an offer was placed on the table for Simon & Schuster's Atria Books to acquire *When God Winks* from Beyond Words.

There was never again a question of having enough books in the stores. Our little book *When God Winks* was on its way, and our partner, Beyond Words, staved off bankruptcy.

❄

Yet we still needed national attention and, in particular, a way to get onto *The Oprah Winfrey Show*.

Every day, Louise and I would pray about finding the proper door to get through. In fact, I would joke that "Oprah Winfrey has more prayers said for her every day than anybody in America. Mostly by us authors trying to get on her show!"

By 2004, three years after *When God Winks* was published, we felt we had made some real progress. I'd been on Fox

News Channel's *Fox & Friends* several times, and those appearances had boosted our visibility the most. Virtually every major religious broadcaster had also given us support.

Still no Oprah.

On the morning of May 9, 2004—for the first time I could remember—I felt a little dejected. Louise and I had just finished our morning prayer time together. I knew that *The Oprah Winfrey Show* would be winding down for summer hiatus in just three weeks.

In my heart, I knew that meant that I'd have to wait until the show started up again in September. My hopes plummeted as I pictured myself, like a little kid, trudging to the end of the line with my baseball cap in hand.

"I don't think we're going to make it this year," I told Louise with a sigh.

She looked at me brightly and said with authority, "If God wants you on that show, He'll find a way!"

I tend to believe everything my wife says. So I nodded, accepted, and, perhaps for the first time, let go and let God.

❄

Three days later, we were driving through Virginia Beach, where we traveled monthly for Louise to tape her talk show, *Living the Life,* on ABC's Family Channel.

My cell phone rang. It was a woman's voice—a friend from our hometown on Martha's Vineyard, breathless with excitement. "Oprah just held up your book!" she blurted out.

My eyes squinted, as if that would somehow help me hear what she had just said. Slowly I shook my head. "Thank you for calling to tell me," I said politely, absolutely certain that she had me confused with someone else.

After hanging up, I shrugged, glanced at Louise, and said, "She must be confused."

Then, within seconds, I got three more calls, including one from Richard Cohn, my first publisher. The same message: "Oprah just held up your book!"

We were astounded. How could that have happened?

✳

Here's what we found out later.

Oprah was giving her TV audience a tour of her Chicago home. Entering a guest bedroom, she mentioned that rather than having a TV in that room, she liked to keep her favorite books by the bed. She reached down, picked up the top book on the pile, and looked back to the camera.

"Here's a book called *When God Winks*—I love that—cute little stories about how there are no coincidences in our life." Then she set the book down and went on with her tour.

✳

On Amazon and Barnes & Noble, there was a flurry of activity. The book shot into the top ten in a matter of hours.

When we returned home and got back into our routine, we sat on the same sofa where, on the previous Friday, we had prayed for a pathway to the attention of decision makers at *The Oprah Winfrey Show*.

I said to Louise that it was the first time I could ever recall expressing disappointment. But only seventy-two hours later, God gave us a Godwink of hope and encouragement.

Wow. How amazing is that?

※

Some people might ask, "How could God get your book into Oprah's bedroom, on her nightstand, just three days after your prayer?"

I say, "It's simple. He's God. That's how!"

※

When we look back upon the twenty-year journey of this new word, "Godwinks," we are awestruck.

Just connect the dots.

- Start with the Godwink of my boyhood hero, Dr. Norman Vincent Peale, being called to Heaven on Christmas Eve and thereby becoming integral to my talk that birthed the Godwinks Thesis.
- Link that to the astonishing Godwink of our being divinely aligned with Judith Curr at Simon & Schuster by a young book buyer at Waldenbooks. Judith was the perfect publisher to take our Godwinks brand to the next level.

- Then connect to God's answering of our persistent prayer to open a door for us at *Oprah*, the most powerful television program of its time, which He did in a manner wilder than anyone's imagination.

When God doesn't answer your prayers in a "timely" manner, you are tempted to ask, "When, God?" But He works on a very different timetable.

When you get into sync with God's calendar, you'll find that He's always putting things into place at the perfect time.

On the other hand, have you noticed that when we go by our own timetables—pushing things to happen—they have a tendency to fall apart?

> *God isn't slow . . . He's always on time.*
> *There is an appointed time for everything.*
> *And there is a time for every event under heaven.*
> —ECCLESIASTES 3:1 (NASB)

REFLECTIONS

The new word in the language—Godwink—signifies "Signs of Hope." It provides a name for the belief that we are part of a much bigger picture. Every Godwink is another stitch in the magnificent tapestry that God is weaving for us.

By acknowledging our Godwinks, we seem to see them more and more. Also, the threads that link one Godwink to the next become more visible, and then we notice an emergence of a whole map of Godwinks. Soon you're aware of how magnificently He has woven pathways to the very people He wants you to meet, putting you and them at the right place at the right time. We call that the Divine Alignment of Godwinks.

❈

The concept of divinely aligned Godwinks that lead you to your perfect mate is exemplified in the next story. The way that Paula and Gery romantically met, married, and developed one of the top five inns in the United States is a real-life fairy tale.

You'll see why their love story was chosen by the Hallmark Channel as the premiere of the Godwinks Movie Series—as of this printing, slated to air at Christmastime 2018.

5

Paula and Gery: A Charlotte Inn Christmas

Gery Conover was a dreamer—the kind of guy who believed that as long as you have to think . . . you might as well think big.

He was also a doer. When he put his mind to something, he pursued it. He finished it. And did it right.

When Gery was eleven, his parents returned home to find that he'd repainted and decorated his room to replicate a suite in an upscale inn—a forecast of things to come.

Years later, Gery and his first wife moved to Martha's Vineyard off the coast of Massachusetts, had two boys, and opened a small art shop in Edgartown, the island's oldest, quaintest community, where they began selling the works of local artists. The marriage did not last, but Gery's love of Martha's Vineyard endured. He spotted a woefully dilapidated inn near the center of town and envisioned how it could be turned into both an elegant inn and a more sizable art shop. He bought it and commenced a painstakingly authentic restoration. The Charlotte Inn opened in 1972 as a beautiful and charming structure, soon becoming one of the top five inns in the United States.

Its brochure describes it this way:

Our gallery offers a glimpse inside one of the world's finest small hotels, The Charlotte Inn of Edgartown on the island of Martha's Vineyard. Here, you may explore its quiet sitting rooms and private passageways, sumptuous guest quarters, and the island's most romantic restaurant, The Terrace. Stroll along meandering brick paths through the inn's English country–style gardens, and admire the meticulously restored buildings and charming Edwardian-era accoutrements.

Gery worked hard. Over time, he began dating again. And to many fair ladies, he was the catch of catches; after all, he looked like a model for Ralph Lauren or *GQ*; he was highly successful and the owner of a romantic inn on one of America's most desired island destinations.

Among his leisure industry colleagues and within the community, Gery's determination to achieve perfection in every aspect of his work and personal life became legendary.

Yet without perfect love, life was not perfect.

❅

Paula, at twenty-nine, the oldest daughter of a fine family from the suburbs of St. Louis, was a strikingly beautiful blonde with a wonderfully wry sense of humor.

From the wedding photos, her marriage seemed like a perfect match.

It was not. The groom was a good man but not a good husband for Paula.

As the marriage dissolved, Paula's dream of finding Prince Charming faded and she focused her attention on another long-held dream: owning an art gift shop.

When a gift market wholesaler in Boston said he would help set her up in business, she scheduled a meeting on the way home from a holiday visit to her dear friend Mary Jane, who lived on the charming island of Nantucket, also off the coast of Massachusetts.

Paula traveled from St. Louis to Nantucket by plane, connecting through Boston. It was always good to see her old friend Mary Jane, who met her at the small island airport. They planned to spend a couple days on Nantucket, which is magical at Christmastime, and then take a day-trip flight to Martha's Vineyard, fifteen miles away, and then spend one final day on Nantucket.

Paula set the meeting with the gift wholesaler on the day she was leaving via Boston.

While driving to the airport for their Vineyard excursion day, Mary Jane told Paula that Edgartown had wonderful art and gift shops and it would be festive and fun.

Then Mary Jane received a call—an urgent work matter that required her to remain on Nantucket. However, she insisted that Paula go on to the Vineyard without her.

"No . . . I'll just wait till next time," said Paula.

"I want you to go," said Mary Jane. "It'll be good for you. And if you're going to be in the art and gift shop business, you need to know about both islands."

But the weather had other plans. They found that Nantucket airport was fogged in and no flights were departing. Still, as long as they were there, they decided to have breakfast in the airport coffee shop.

✳

As Paula and Mary Jane were finishing breakfast, an announcement came over the loudspeaker that the fog had lifted. The flight to Martha's Vineyard was leaving right away.

"Go. Go and grab that plane," Mary Jane told Paula.

"No, why don't I just stay here," Paula said weakly, but she knew she couldn't prevail against Mary Jane when her mind was made up.

As Paula rushed to the gate, Mary Jane promised to pick her up on the late-afternoon flight back to Nantucket.

"Have fun," she directed, smiling and waving as Paula boarded the small plane.

✳

At Martha's Vineyard, Paula was unable to locate any cabs. She asked a man in the office of the airport manager how to get to Edgartown.

"Well, because of the fog, cabs weren't waitin' around," drawled the man in a New England accent. Then, lifting a nearby casement window, he shouted to a fellow standing beside his car outside the little terminal. "Gery! Can you give this girl a ride to town?"

Turning back to Paula, he explained that on the island, people help each other out: "He's Gery Conover, an innkeeper in Edgartown. He'll give you a lift."

Paula looked at the handsome man dressed in khakis and a white shirt with rolled-up sleeves standing next to a white Corvette convertible.

"I could do worse," Paula told herself.

Introductions made, Gery said he would be glad to give Paula a lift—he had just been seeing a friend off on the same plane that Paula had arrived on.

As Gery chatted with Paula about Edgartown and Martha's Vineyard, exuding pride for the island, he became more and more captivated by her. He took her to some of his favorite art and antiques shops along the narrow streets of Edgartown. He was particularly impressed with her knowledge of art and artists.

He took her for a ride in his Boston Whaler, a classic-looking boat, down Katama Bay past all the mansions, then over to the Chappy Beach Club on the adjacent Chappaquiddick Island.

Saving the best for last, he took her to the elegant Charlotte Inn for afternoon tea.

Paula was impressed. "I could *live* in a place like this!" she said with awe.

"Why don't you stay over? We have rooms available," said Gery. "I could show you up island tomorrow."

"No, no. I have to be back in Nantucket tonight," said Paula. "My friend is meeting me at the airport."

"You could go back tomorrow," pressed Gery.

"No . . . no . . . I couldn't."

"You know, we have fog sometimes in late afternoon," said Gery. "Let me check the airport."

When he called the airport, his heart leaped to hear "All planes at Martha's Vineyard Airport are grounded. A fog front has just come in."

Gery returned to Paula's table. He had a sad-but-not-too-sad look on his face. "I'm sorry," he said, pressing his lips together to keep from smiling. "The airport is fogged in."

❆

As Paula examined the decor in her room, marveling at the care that had gone into the selection and placement of every item, mostly valuable antiques, she had a growing appreciation for the talents of the man whose path she had been placed into by the Godwink of fog. She reflected on the day's nonstop conversation. How easy it had been. How interested he had been in what *she* had to say, *her* opinions. He seemed to like her sense of humor, too.

❆

Through the years Gery Conover had developed a keen eye for the beautiful things in life. He had spent years looking at paintings, fine antiques, and other rare valuables.

Long ago he had learned that when you see something of exceptional value, you must go for it. Doggedly. Don't wait. It might not be there when you come back.

Paula was neither a magnificent painting nor a priceless jewel; but she was a beautiful human being—a beautiful woman in whose company and by whose easy conversation he had been captivated for an entire day. He realized he was a player in a divinely aligned series of events and timing that had placed him in the perfect place at the perfect time—waiting outside the airport. Something unexpected and unavoidable had happened. He was in love.

❄

Paula called her friend Mary Jane on Nantucket. "We're fogged in. I have to stay the night," she said in a disappointed tone of voice, hoping she didn't sound transparent.

"Funny, it's clear as a bell here!" exclaimed Mary Jane.

❄

The next day Gery advised Paula that the only flight back to Nantucket would be late in the afternoon, so he again orchestrated a full day of countryside tours in the Corvette, with the top down.

By midafternoon he was again inviting her to stay—"just one more day."

"No, no, I *have* to go," she protested. "I don't want to, but I have to."

She explained that she had to gather her baggage in Nantucket and then depart for her meeting with the gift wholesaler in Boston the following morning.

Sadly, Gery drove her to the airport. Seeing Paula's plane lift into the sky gave him a deeper feeling of loss than he had ever before experienced. He stood riveted, trying to keep the tiny plane in focus for as long as possible, until it disappeared into the clouds.

❄

Paula arrived at her appointment in Boston the next morning and greeted Tony, the gift market wholesaler, whom she had spoken with by phone from St. Louis, reiterating her plan to start a gift shop back home. He suggested that they could either talk in the office or, seeing that it was lunchtime, why not talk over lunch? He suggested a restaurant, but on the way out of the building, he decided to take her to a different one.

At some point during lunch, the waitress came to the table and asked if her name was Paula.

"Yes," Paula replied, puzzled.

"There's a phone call for you."

"Did you tell anyone where we were going for lunch?" Paula asked Tony as she got up to go to the phone.

Tony shook his head.

"Hi, Paula, this is Gery," said the voice on the phone.

"How . . . how in the world did you track me down?" gasped Paula.

Gery explained that he had been doing some detective work all morning long, checking one wholesaler after another, until he had reached the desk of one secretary who confirmed that her boss was having lunch with a pretty blond lady and might have taken her to one of several of his favorite restaurants. He kept calling until he reached the right one.

Gery then began entreating Paula to come back to Martha's Vineyard instead of returning to St. Louis.

"No, no, I can't," said Paula, wearing an astonished smile. "I really must go back home. I have dogs . . . I have commitments I need to keep . . ."

Finally, she firmly stated that she had to get back to her meeting. Returning to the table, she apologetically explained what had happened.

After lunch, Paula had to rush to the airport in order to catch her late-afternoon flight to St. Louis. Arriving at the gate just a few minutes before departure, she joined the line of people who were starting to board. Something caught her attention. It was her name being spoken. She turned. The loudspeaker was saying her name and asking her to pick up a courtesy phone. Fortunately, there was one on the wall close to where she was standing.

"Hi, Paula, it's Gery."

Breathless with surprise and buoyed by his charm, Paula found herself repeating an all-too-familiar phrase: "No, no, I can't. I really do have to go back."

"Come back to Martha's Vineyard, just for the rest of the week," implored Gery. He explained that he had been calling the airport every ten minutes, telling the people that it was an emergency and he had to reach her.

The man at the door of the plane was now signaling Paula. All the other passengers had boarded. "Are you coming?" he mouthed to her.

"Yes, just a minute," she mouthed back.

"Let me tell you about another plane that will take you back to the Vineyard," continued Gery.

"No . . . no . . ."

"Are you coming, ma'am, or not?" insisted the flight attendant, having walked over to her, putting his face within inches of hers.

Paula paused. Perhaps a second. Maybe a millisecond.

"No, I am *not* coming!" she stated firmly—to the flight attendant.

❄

Joy leaped within Gery's chest.

"Here's what you do," he excitedly instructed. "Find your way to Butler Aviation—those are private airplanes— there will be a plane there for you in forty-five minutes."

In forty-five minutes a chartered plane rolled up to the

Butler hangar. Paula expected to see a pilot deplane. Instead, she felt a tingle as the steps lowered and she saw Gery Conover climbing down. He hugged Paula and helped her into the plane. Soon they were airborne, heading back to Martha's Vineyard.

For three days Gery and Paula talked about everything. They felt with certainty that they were meant for each other. They sensed that powerful unseen forces were unfolding a design for their lives that was meant to be.

"How much time do you need to wrap things up in St. Louis?" asked Gery.

"Two weeks," replied Paula.

Gery smiled. "How about one?"

❄

During the following week Paula entered into a whirlwind of reconstruction for her life—pulling up every thread of connection in St. Louis to move to an island off the coast of Massachusetts. To help her to remain confident, Gery telephoned, several times every day.

When Paula overpacked her car for the drive to Massachusetts and had no room for her dog carriers, she broke down crying.

The phone rang. It was Gery. "I don't have any room for my little dogs," she cried. "I don't know what to do. I have to bring them with me."

"Don't worry about a thing," said Gery calmly. "Do you have someone who can take the dogs just for tonight?"

"Yes," she said softly, holding back sniffles.

"Here's what you do. Take your dogs to your friend. Drive your car to the airport. Leave the car with valet parking. Tell them that a man named Kincade will pick it up tomorrow. Go to the ticket counter. There are prepaid tickets there for you."

He explained that he would send one of his workers to St. Louis the next day, have him pick up the car and the dogs, drive Paula's car back to Woods Hole, Massachusetts, and catch the car ferry to Martha's Vineyard.

❋

A few months later, like a romantic Cary Grant and Audrey Hepburn movie where the fog lifts, the music swells, and two soul mates embrace, Gery and Paula came together as husband and wife in a small ceremony at one of the most idyllic spots on Earth: the private quarters of their very own Charlotte Inn on Martha's Vineyard. As the bride and groom looked through the charming small-paned windows into a magnificent English garden, traces of mist began to emerge—a reminder that the divine Maker of all things perfect is the author of perfect love. He is also the creator of perfectly timed fog—as Godwinks.

❄

Today Paula looks back upon her decision with clarity: "I knew the moment I spoke those words to the flight attendant—'No, I am *not* coming'—that I was not just curtailing a trip to St. Louis. I was making a much bigger decision—the right one—for the rest of my life."

"It's amazing," says Gery, reflecting on almost four decades of happy marriage. "In all those years we've never had a single argument. We're together, running the inn, almost every moment of every day. Yet when she goes to the grocery store—I miss her."

❄

If you felt that Paula and Gery's love story seemed like a romantic Christmas movie on the Hallmark Channel, you're in good company. As mentioned earlier, the executives at Hallmark felt the same way and selected it as the first of the Godwinks Movie Series.

REFLECTIONS
Each of us has a destiny. It's like our DNA. It's there. We're born with it.

But we also believe that God allows us to have our hands on the steering wheel most of the way through life—we can go too fast or too slow or recklessly drive off a cliff and never reach our intended destiny. That's free will.

In our speaking engagements, Louise and I will often

make this promise: "You cannot sit on your baggage, beside the road, waiting for your destiny to come to you. You must get up, leave your baggage behind, and head for what you believe to be your destiny. And once you do, look for the signposts along the way—the Godwinks. Those are the messages of reassurance, directly from above, that you're heading in the right direction."

❇

In Paula and Gery's story, it was the divine alignment of weather conditions and Godwinks that placed both of them at the right place at the right time.

However, if they—particularly Gery—had not stepped out in faith and "gone for" what they believed to be their destiny, their love story might never have materialized.

The gift of lasting love that they found waiting for them when they pursued their destiny was priceless.

6

Tonya: Christmas Aprons

Tonya Rohr loves shoes. Or, as she says, "Shoes and shoes and shoes."

She also loves aprons. In fact, you could say that she probably needs separate closets just for shoes and aprons.

Tonya and her husband, Devin, are known as the funny members of the ministry team at the Assembly in Broken Arrow, Oklahoma. They're associate pastors and lead the Sunday-morning Bible studies on families.

A week or two before Christmas, Tonya was given two gifts. Both were aprons, from two dear friends, Kay and Lana.

"One was the cutest pink-and-white-striped apron reminding me of a candy striper's smock. Remember those?"

She says that when she was a girl she used to volunteer as a candy striper at the hospital, delivering flowers and newspapers to patients. The uniform had pink and white stripes, reminiscent of a candy cane.

"The apron Kay gave me had a perfect quote embroidered on the front bib. It said, 'Will cook for shoes,' and along the bottom it read, 'Lots and lots of shoes!'" She laughs. The only trouble was, the apron felt a little too short.

The second apron, from Lana, was black with white polka dots; it fit perfectly. "It had white piping along the bottom and on the pocket was my initial, 'R.' It was way cute."

She graciously and excitedly thanked Kay and Lana and added the new aprons to her collection.

The following December, again just before Christmas, Tonya and Devin were heading to church. As they rode along, Tonya's mind, for some reason, flashed back to those two aprons. She had now favored both of them for an entire year.

"I thought about my pink-and-white one and how cute it was. Then I thought about my black one and how well it fit—and how I liked the piping."

As they drove, she continued to fantasize. *Wouldn't it be wonderful if I could put the two aprons together? I'd take the black-and-white apron with the piping and meld it with the pink-and-white one, adding the funny quote about shoes.*

Poof. As quickly as the thought had entered her mind, it vanished.

She and Devin had arrived at church and were entering the back door. She saw her friend MarLynn waving her into the kitchen. A group of ladies was gathered there. They all hugged.

MarLynn then reached behind her and handed Tonya a small bag. "This is for you from Mom and me. Merry Christmas!"

Tonya knew that MarLynn's mother was a talented seamstress. "Oh my!" she said, looking at the package. "Thank you!" She loved surprises, and this surely counted as one!

She reached into the package and was overwhelmed by what she saw: a black apron with hot pink piping and the words "Will cook for shoes!" embroidered on the bib! She was speechless. The ladies looking back at her had no idea that only moments before, she had been daydreaming about that very apron!

"It flashed through my mind that I had never before thought those thoughts about combining my pink and black aprons, yet here I was, holding my fantasy in my hands! Including the quote about shoes!"

With a smile and a twinkle in her eyes, Tonya adds, "*That*, my friends, is a Godwink."

REFLECTIONS

What Tonya presumed was a random thought entering her mind—how perfect it would be if those two aprons were blended together—was actually God in action. In a fleeting moment He was placing the desire in her heart, and she was sending Him an unarticulated prayer. He then caused the Godwink to follow.

Nothing is too small or big for God to do. Many people don't pray about things because they feel they're not worth His time. Perhaps you feel that something is of too little significance to God. But everything is important to Him.

Just look at the colors in a bird, the foot of a baby, the petals of a flower. He is interested in every detail of everything in the universe—and everything in your life. He's a God of detail.

The ancient scriptures tell us that even the hairs of your head are numbered by Him. No prayer request is too small. He already knows what is on your heart and mind. You may forget that you prayed for something, but God never forgets. Not one prayer is wasted. Not one prayer is forgotten.

How did God read Tonya's thoughts and desires about the two aprons? Simple . . . He's a great mind reader!

7

Gerry: A Christmas of Second Chances

Christmastime in New Orleans is always festive. It's like one long celebration from Thanksgiving to New Year's.

Decorations drape the wrought-iron deck railings of historic French Quarter homes and hotels, creating a scene that looks like an etching from Charles Dickens's *A Christmas Carol*, celebrating the light and the love of the season.

Yet the crusaders of darkness have strong representation in this charming city as well. They assemble in rowdy bars, long into the night, and the true meaning of Christmas rarely crosses their minds and lips.

Prior to this day, three weeks before Christmas, Gerry Ponson, a forty-four-year-old with a rugged face and a silver brush cut, was among the latter.

❄

"Hold on, Mac . . . I'm not going to leave you!" shouted Gerry, the younger of the two men struggling to keep their heads above water.

"I'm cold . . . I don't think I can hold on any longer!" Mac was shivering, his lips blue from the frigid December waters.

"Just keep hanging on to that pole!" shouted Gerry. "It'll be light soon . . . somebody'll see us." Gerry tried desperately to believe his own words.

Gerry Ponson, along with his older friend Mac Ansespy and Mac's dog, Booga, a golden retriever, had left shore at 5 a.m. to cross the three-mile bay near New Orleans to their favorite duck-hunting spot.

Gerry earned his living as a seasoned fisherman. He knew these waters like the back of his hand. You go out a mile-and-a-half, and the waters stay eight to ten feet deep. Then they suddenly drop off into a deep channel. That allows the big boats and ships to cruise up the bay.

The forecast had called for nasty weather, but Gerry lived dangerously. He thought that if they got their seventeen-foot open-bay boat across early enough, they could make it. That's what he told Mac. But as they neared the edge of the deep abyss, the waters became increasingly choppy; a northwester suddenly charged up the channel, bearing down on them with five- and six-foot waves, tossing their craft like a toy.

Gerry had let Mac drive the boat. When seawater splashed over them, Mac momentarily took his hands from the steering wheel to clean his glasses. In that instant, the rough waters seized the boat, causing it to move sideways in the waves.

"Turn the boat, turn the boat!" Gerry shouted, but it was too late. A huge wave crashed in on them, instantly filling their vessel, sinking it in eight feet of water.

One of the few items that Gerry could grab was a ten-foot push pole used for moving a boat through shallower waters. By plunging the stick into the mud and standing on the gunwales of the boat, they could just keep their heads and shoulders above water.

"Grab that pole, Mac, and hold on!" Gerry yelled.

Gerry knew Mac was in no shape to swim to shore. Besides, until the sun came up, they might be swimming in circles. He also considered leaving Mac and swimming for help. But that wouldn't work. Even if he made it ashore, it was five miles to the nearest phone. And Mac couldn't survive on his own. No . . . all they could do was wait—and hope for a boat to come up that channel.

For two hours Gerry would alternately prop up Mac, then grab the dog by the collar and help him stay afloat for a few minutes.

Finally, Gerry felt he had no choice but to make a decision. He told the dog to go.

"Where's Booga?" gasped Mac, disoriented after so long in the water, looking around for his champion dog.

"I tol' him to git. I can save you, Mac, but I can't save you both."

In his heart he knew the dog would never make it. A mile-and-a-half back to shore in those nasty waters would be too much for any creature.

Gerry's constant movement was helping him stave off hypothermia, but Mac's body temperature, he surmised, was plunging dangerously low. He could see that the frigid waters and biting wind were starting to cause a shutdown of Mac's body functions.

"I'm cold, Gerry . . . I can't hold on any longer," Mac panted, mentally letting go as well.

"Hold on, Mac. Somebody'll come."

Gerry didn't really believe that.

He didn't believe in anything. He'd been a heathen all his adult life. There were times as a kid when he kinda believed God existed; everybody said so, but he was a kid—what did he know? When he grew up, he couldn't see the use of God. "He's just a crutch," he'd often say, pontificating to some drunk at one of those beer joints he liked to frequent in New Orleans.

With a derisive sneer, and speaking a little too loud, he'd say, "I got religion, all right! I worship wine, women, and song!" He'd laugh at his own joke.

Gerry had to hand it to his sister. She tried. Over and over, she attempted to talk to him about God. He'd have nothing of it. He once called her a fruitcake and told her to "get her blankety-blank outta his house."

Smash!

A wave drenched him.

"Hold on, Mac!"

Given his present situation, he wondered if he should have listened to his sister.

His girlfriend, Shannon, was one of those "believers" too. Still, she didn't press him like his sister did. Shannon gave him space. But, truth be known, she'd be a lot happier if he fell into line, accepting what she accepted.

He shook his head. He just couldn't bring himself to do that.

"I can't hold on anymore," said Mac, weaker now.

Smash! Another wave.

"Yes you can! Hold on!" encouraged Gerry, trying to buy his own baloney. But this was bad. Really bad.

He was beginning to see the inevitable. In well over two hours, not one single boat had come up that channel. That meant that no boats were out in this weather. And *that* meant their chances were slim to none.

We're gonna die out here. Nobody's comin' . . . we're gonna die, he began to say to himself.

Gerry lifted his eyes to the low-hanging, gray, overcast sky. *What if I were to talk to God? What would I say? How would I say it?*

Smash! The waves were feeling colder now. Mac was starting to go limp.

He decided he had nothing to lose.

"God . . . if you hear me . . ." he shouted, his voice cracking. "Please, please send us a boat, God. Give me a second chance, God. That's all I ask. A second chance."

His own words startled him. He couldn't believe what he—Gerry Ponson—had just said.

For the next two minutes he kept his trap shut, listening to the wind, ducking the waves. Occasionally yelling for Mac to hold on, he wondered if God bothered listening to worthless heathens.

Something in the mist made him blink! He blinked repeatedly.

"Mac . . . do you see that?"

Gerry could make out—faintly—what looked like a cross.

"What's that in the channel, Mac?"

Mac didn't respond.

"Mac!" His voice became louder. "That's the mast of a boat, Mac! Coming up the channel!" He started to make it out . . . the silhouette of a big boat, probably seventy-five feet long.

"Hold on to me, Mac! I need to use the pole!"

Trying to get a footing on the gunnels of the sunken

boat as Mac held on to his waist, Gerry pulled the pole from the mud, tore off his jacket, attached it to the end, and waved it frantically in the air.

"Over here! Over here!" Gerry shouted repeatedly.

Doubtful thoughts rushed into his mind.

Who'd be looking off into the mist? Who'd see us—just blobs in rough waters?

"Make 'em see us, God!" shouted Gerry, now in-for-a-penny-and-in-for-a-pound with the Almighty.

"Mac . . . that boat stopped! I think they see us! But it's too big to get over here. It's not deep enough where we are."

Then Gerry saw that someone had leaped from the boat and was swimming toward them.

"They're coming, Mac, they're coming! Hold on!" Gerry was almost giddy with excitement.

A man swam up to them. He told Mac to lie on his back so that he could pull him the hundred yards or so to the boat. On his own, Gerry began swimming alongside the other two men.

It hadn't yet sunk in that within minutes of asking God for help, a boat actually showed up. But as Gerry got to the big boat and started climbing the rope ladder, he saw something that struck him like a ton of bricks.

He knew right then and there that God existed. No doubt about it. He'd heard his pleading prayer. And it was He who saved him.

What Gerry saw was the name on the side of the boat. It was *Second Chance.*

That's unbelievable!

The owners of the boat—a husband and wife—introduced themselves. It was Karen who had spotted them out there in the fog, and her husband, Bubba, was the one who jumped in to rescue Mac. They gave them dry clothes and blankets.

Wrapped in a wool blanket, Gerry continued to encourage his older friend. "We're going to get you back on shore, Mac. They'll get you to the hospital . . . take good care of you."

Mac was not doing so well. He complained of chest pains.

As Karen and Gerry attended to Mac, Bubba quickly got on the radio, shouting into it, "Mayday! Mayday!"

A voice crackled over the radio. It was the Coast Guard. Soon a flapping sound could be heard and a medevac chopper was overhead. It lowered a medic on a rope, who placed Mac into a sling and pulled him up.

It was an emergency. They couldn't take the time to lift Gerry into the chopper as well. They wanted to get Mac to the hospital right away.

Bubba assured Gerry he'd put him ashore as quickly as possible. He also radioed his brother to meet them, to give Gerry a lift to his pickup truck. Gerry could then go to the hospital to check on Mac.

❋

The skies were clear now. As Gerry drove to the hospital, the power of what had happened that day—the near-death tragedy and the miracle rescue—raced through his mind. A flood of tears was triggered, causing Gerry to pull off the road. Placing his head on his arms on the steering wheel, he couldn't stop saying, "Thank you, God. Thank you."

Gerry eventually looked up and saw that he had pulled off on the side of a causeway. There were lush green marshlands on both sides, as far as you could see. The green, waving grasses blended with the marine-blue skies, sprinkled with puffy white clouds.

It occurred to him that he had traveled this road a thousand times, yet never once had he noticed how spectacular that view was.

"God, your creations sure are beautiful," said Gerry. He once was blind, but now could see. "How could I have doubted you, God, thinkin' all this was just an accident?"

Glancing at his watch, he decided he'd better get going. Checking his side-view mirror, Gerry pulled his truck back onto the causeway.

❋

His old friend Mac looked pretty groggy from all the medication he'd had. Gerry was surprised Mac even knew he was there.

"Did you find Booga?" whispered Mac.

Gerry sadly shook his head. He knew the dog couldn't have made it. But he wanted to give his friend some encouragement.

"When I leave here, Mac, I'm gonna try to find him. I'll promise you that."

"He's a champion," uttered Mac.

"I know," said Gerry, remembering how proudly Mac had announced that Booga was voted third in the nation in his class.

In the hospital parking lot Gerry climbed into his

truck, trying to think of where along the miles and miles of marshy shoreline he could search for any sign of the remains of Booga. It was a hopeless task.

He just started driving back in the direction he'd come from. Soon he was again crossing the causeway over the marshlands. Now driving in the opposite direction, he looked across traffic and saw the spot where he'd pulled his truck over earlier. Gerry broke down in tears, declaring that from now on God was going to be the Captain. He— Gerry—would be just the first mate.

At that moment, he was approaching an exit. He decided to pull off. A narrow ramp led down to a dirt road adjacent to the marshlands.

Gerry drove slowly. With the windows down in the truck, he could smell the sweet, fresh sea air blended with a fishy odor.

Where would I start looking for the body of a lost dog? he thought. *Talk about a needle in a haystack.*

He pulled the truck over and stopped. He had a revelation. Once before on that day something very unusual had happened. He'd actually prayed. Asking God for help. And God answered that prayer. Why not try it again? If God gave him one miracle, how about two?

"God, if I can please ask for one more second chance, sir? Could I ask that you give Booga a second chance?"

Then he sat quietly for a few minutes, marveling at the

sounds of nature—gulls, frogs, crickets, owls—as if he were hearing them for the first time.

That's when he heard it. Faintly. Then louder.

Woof!

Gerry stiffened. Every sense was on alert.

Woof! Woof!

"Booga! Is that you?" He jumped out of the truck.

Mac's champion golden retriever came bounding up to him, covering Gerry's face with excited dog kisses!

Tears welled up in Gerry's eyes. Twice in one day. He couldn't believe that! God was offering second chances twice in one day!

Gerry laughed and laughed as he tried to pet his enthusiastic friend. "I know what you're saying, Booga . . . you're sayin', 'Hey, where ta' heck have you been? I've been waitin' out here for hours.'"

He watched the dog wag his tail rapidly.

"Booga, you really *are* a champion, boy! Wow! And so are you, God!"

He hugged the dog one more time. "Let's go for a ride, Booga. Let's surprise Mac!"

Booga didn't need a second invitation. He leaped up into the truck, taking the passenger's seat next to Gerry.

❄

Gerry Ponson experienced a major transformation in his life. It was emblazoned on his heart and mind that a boat named *Second Chance* had been delivered to him through prayer, just as he was giving up all hope.

Gerry committed himself to serving his Maker for the rest of his life. And ever since, he's been a New Orleans street preacher working with Celebration Church.

If you ever get the opportunity to meet him, don't bother trying to convince him that prayer doesn't work. He knows differently!

❄

Eleven days after Gerry was lifted from the cold waters in the bay, he walked along the green-and-red–decorated streets of the French Quarter in New Orleans.

Passing one old hangout after another, he felt he'd been somehow rebirthed.

He *was*, actually—he was on his way to Christmas Eve services at church, arm in arm with his girlfriend, Shannon.

Wanting to make everything right with the Lord, and to start the New Year off with a clean slate, he asked Shannon that evening to marry him—the following week, on December 30th. She smiled, said yes, and hugged him.

That was the best Christmas and New Year's that Gerry can ever remember.

✳

Were he still a gambler, which he wasn't, he'd have said, "What are the odds of getting two incredible Godwink second chances in one day?"

Don't bother trying to compute that.

REFLECTIONS

Gerry was lost in the pleasures of this world, oblivious that his lifestyle was a recipe for disaster.

It took some serious dunking in frigid waters to snap him back to reality.

Life's journey is not always smooth or perfect. There are bumps and detours, and sometimes even collisions, that bring us to a screeching halt.

Even though you may have wandered off into dangerous waters, God will be your life preserver.

Follow Gerry's example; call out to God. He's listening. He'll hear you and give you the gift of a second chance. Gerry is a walking, talking example of that!

> *Here I am! I stand at the door and knock.*
> *If you hear my voice and open the door,*
> *I will come in.*
>
> —REVELATION 3:20 (NCV)

8

Frank: Chocolate Chip Cookie Trips for Kids

Frank Squeo has always loved chocolate chip cookies. One of his fondest Christmas memories as a kid was joining his mother in the kitchen, tying on an apron, and baking cookies together.

He followed that practice after he got his master's degree in finance and started several companies. Each Christmas he dons his apron, bakes cookies, and delivers them to clients.

There are two more things about Frank that you'll appreciate: One, he visits Disney World whenever possible because he loves to see the joy on the faces of children. In fact, during one recent year he walked through the turnstiles forty times. Two, Frank has been a dyed-in-the-wool New York Yankees fan since childhood.

That's where this Godwink story really begins. Forty years ago, Frank and his buddy Bob would buy packages of seventeen tickets to Yankee games for ten bucks a game.

Way up there in the upper deck, they weren't flashy seats, but they got to cheer for their Yanks!

One of the drawbacks of Frank and Bob's seats was that they were directly below a railing that ran along an aisle that was used by soft drink vendors. Those fellas had the annoying habit of resting their heavy carriers, loaded with drinks, on that railing. The cups would splash over the sides, dousing Frank and Bob, in the seats below, with sticky liquid.

Eventually, Frank decided to do something about it. Before buying his tickets for the next season, he looked up the name of the man who was in charge of tickets in the front office at Yankee headquarters. He wrote a friendly letter to Mr. Frank Swaine explaining the situation. To Frank's pleasant surprise, when the tickets came back in the mail, they had been moved down a row, out of harm's way.

It didn't stop there. For the next two years, Frank sent notes to Mr. Swaine—a right-hand man of Yankees owner George Steinbrenner—thanking him for how nice he'd been. Mr. Swaine, as a result, took an interest in the two rabid Yankees fans and kept moving them down until they were in the front row, upper deck.

From that day forward, Frank and Bob enjoyed their Yankee seats immensely.

※

Fast-forward twenty-five years.

One day Frank was chatting with his neighbor Gina.

She told him she wanted to share some exciting news that he, more than anyone else, would appreciate. She had just accepted a new job: working for the Yankees organization.

"Wow! You are so fortunate, Gina!" exclaimed Frank.

"Why don't you meet me in the city sometime? I'll give you a tour of Yankees headquarters, then we'll go for lunch," she suggested.

"I'd love that!" said Frank, naming a date the following week, when he was planning to be in NYC.

Frank was elated. As far as he was concerned, getting to see the inner workings of Yankees headquarters was better than a presidential tour of the White House or a stroll through Buckingham Palace led by the queen herself.

Frank was awestruck as he arrived at Yankees headquarters. He absorbed every detail. He studied the photos of some of his greatest heroes that lined the walls. He gazed at pictures of coaches he'd admired for years. And when

Gina pointed to the big office of Yankees owner George Steinbrenner, he couldn't believe it.

Close to that office, Gina showed Frank where she worked.

At that moment, her boss emerged from his office. She greeted him, saying, "This is my neighbor Frank Squeo." Looking at Frank, she said, "Please meet my wonderful boss, Mr. Frank Swaine."

"Mr. Swaine?" said Frank, wide-eyed and dumb-founded. "Oh . . . it's nice to meet you. I had no idea that Gina worked for you, sir."

Mr. Swaine smiled at Frank and extended a hand. With a pensive look on his face, he asked, "Were you that young man who wrote letters to me years ago, asking me to move your seats so you wouldn't get splashed with soda?"

They all laughed.

Frank nodded and smiled. Inside, he was blown away that such an important man would remember him from so long ago.

"It's nice to meet you, Frank," said the older man. "How have your seats been lately?"

"Wonderful," said Frank. "Just wonderful."

❋

That turned out to be one of Frank's most memorable days and one of the biggest Godwinks in his life. For weeks he couldn't stop talking about it.

And the more he talked about it, the more he marveled

at what had happened. *What are the chances that my neighbor Gina would be my ticket to the thrill of a lifetime?*

Little did he know that God was not yet finished winking at him.

❋

Five years later, in conversation with Gina, he told her about a strange lump that had recently appeared on his neck. "I've seen two doctors, and they don't know what it is," he said, sounding a little worried.

The next day at work, Gina's boss, out of the blue, asked, "How's your friend Frank?"

Pleasantly surprised, she replied, "I just saw him yesterday, Mr. Swaine. He's fine, but . . . just a little worried about an odd lump on his neck."

"Really?" replied Mr. Swaine, narrowing his eyes. He reached for a pad of paper and wrote down a name and number. Speaking deliberately, he handed it to Gina. "Tell Frank to go to Sloan Kettering and meet with this doctor right away."

Frank entered the famous New York cancer hospital the next day. Dr. Richard Wong greeted him graciously, smiling as he said, "I don't know who you know, Frank, but my boss said, 'Get him in here right away.' "

After several tests, Dr. Wong, a specialist in head and neck cancer, connected Frank with one of the world's top specialists on testicular cancer, Dr. George Bosl. Frank was subsequently advised by Dr. Bosl that he was suffering from advanced stage III testicular cancer that had spread throughout his body. That explained the lump on his neck. He had two surgeries right away and subsequently began an aggressive regimen of chemotherapy, five hours a day for the next three months.

As Frank endured his weekly chemo treatments at Westchester Medical Center, he had plenty of time to think things over. He had countless reasons to be grateful for everything that had transpired. How was it that Mr. Swaine had suspected that the lump on his neck might be cancerous and connected him to a renowned New York doctor right away? Who would have thought a lump on the neck would be associated with testicular cancer? And now Dr. Bosl was optimistic that they'd caught it in time! And this had all started with sticky spilled soda?

He chuckled at God's amazing ways. Then his thoughts turned serious: *I know there's some reason why everything in my life has lined up.*

As Frank looked around at the other patients in the hospital, he saw no smiles. He was heartbroken to see children going through the same kind of treatment he was. Many had lost their hair. Most had vacant looks on their faces. A smile was rare.

During the endless hours he spent hooked up to the

chemo machine, Frank's entrepreneurial mind kept on working, and an idea began to blossom. *What would make these kids smile?* he pondered.

He thought about what had given him joy through the years. He thought about the Yankees. Then he focused on chocolate chip cookies and trips to Disney World. Those thoughts became the two pillars on which his big idea was beginning to hang.

As soon as he was able to, Frank registered a nonprofit organization called "Baking Memories 4 Kids."

This was the plan: Each year, about a month before Christmas, he would amass a small army of three hundred volunteers to bake thousands of chocolate chip cookies. They would be sold to raise funds to send terminally ill kids and their families on all-expense-paid trips to major amusement parks in Orlando.

❄

How did Frank's big idea do?

It keeps on getting bigger. After its first five years in operation, Baking Memories 4 Kids sold over a million cookies for Christmas. Funds were raised to send forty-six kids and their families to Florida, up from seventeen kids and families the year before.

What is Frank's greatest satisfaction?

The beaming smiles on the faces of little children.

Looking at Frank's journey as a tapestry of events, we can see how God threaded numerous Godwinks together to touch many lives in profound ways:

1. Drinks spilled by careless vendors at Yankee Stadium prompted Frank to step out in faith.

2. That resulted in better Yankee seats, but more importantly, made him visible to Yankees executive Frank Swaine.
3. A neighbor named Gina "happened" to get a job working for Frank Swaine.
4. The two Franks were divinely aligned to meet.
5. Information from one Frank averted a medical crisis for the other Frank.
6. A nonprofit to create smiles for terminally ill children was the outcome of all those Godwinks.

REFLECTIONS

Frank Squeo was getting early clues directly from the Holy Spirit when he pondered, *I know there's some reason why everything in my life has lined up.*

How would *you* live your life if you believed—as Frank does—that your life is not a series of random, unrelated events but that every thread plays a vital role, woven into a perfect design that is beautiful and purposeful?

When God puts a dream into your heart, He will fulfill it.

In all things, God works for the good
of those who love him,
who have been called according to his purpose.

—ROMANS 8:28 (NIV)

9

Roma: The Job of a
Christmas Angel

As the lead angel on the popular TV series *Touched by an Angel*, seen by twenty-one million viewers every week, Roma Downey learned that she had been given a special opportunity to lift the spirits of people but that in real life the job also carried unique responsibilities.

"When you play an angel on TV, some people think you *are* an angel in real life," says Roma sweetly, with a warm Irish lilt that implies that you and she are lifelong friends, though you've never met. "Sometimes, when people met me, they would speak reverently, as if they were in the presence of someone holy."[1]

Permitting that to sink in for a moment, she smiles from an angelic face framed by soft auburn hair, a trademark of her ancestry. "We all have the opportunity to be an angel if we are just willing to show kindness and grace and love to those around us."

She communicates from a heart bearing the strong faith that she lives by.

※

One day, during a Christmas break from the television series, Roma visited a children's hospital. Walking the corridors wearing a red-and-white Santa cap, she wanted to do her part in bringing a ray of hope to little ones and their hurting families.

She felt that investing the time to have a picture taken with a child who was hospitalized for Christmas would leave them with something more than a smile for the camera—a snapshot they could carry in their hearts long after.

As Roma approached one room, a family was just exiting, holding on to one another. She could tell in a moment what had happened. "You could feel the grief, like a gust of wind out of that room," she says.

Respectfully, she pulled the Santa cap from her head and stepped into a corner.

The mother's face was contorted in pain and anguish. Roma's heart cried out for her.

As their eyes met, the mother's expression transformed into a look of hope, indicating that she knew exactly who Roma was. The woman quickly stepped toward her.

"I prayed that an angel would come for my baby," whispered the mother, "and here you are."

Roma wanted to say, "No, you're wrong. I'm not really an angel, I'm an actress who plays an angel." But her lips failed to move. She looked deeply into those reddened eyes above the tear-streaked cheeks and remained silent. Instead she placed an arm around the mother and whispered, "Let me pray with you."

Standing there in the hospital corridor, they prayed. Words of comfort flowed from Roma's lips, but—she said later—they were not from her; they were words bathed by the grace of God.

Then, with her hands extending to the mother's shoulders, she smiled tenderly and said, "God be with you."

Wiping away a tear that had formed at the corner of her eye, the mother expressed deep-felt gratitude. "Thank you, thank you so much."

Roma left the hospital with mixed feelings. She felt she had tried to do the right thing. Still, she was oppressed by a heavy feeling of guilt. "My heart was beating fast, overwhelmed with emotion . . . questioning whether I had been dishonest. That woman needed an angel, and all she got was me."[2]

She felt that she had somehow permitted herself to become an actor on the stage of real life, leading a mourning mother to believe that she was something that she was not.

As soon as she could, she telephoned her dear friend, fellow actor, and confidante Della Reese. She was the one Roma always turned to for words of encouragement.

"I feel like such a fraud," she said into the phone after explaining what had happened.

"Why would you feel like that?" asked Della compassionately.

"Because that poor woman was in a vulnerable place and needed support. I allowed her to think that God had sent *me* there to provide it for her."

"And who says He didn't?" asked Della matter-of-factly. Then, with calm authority, she added, "Baby, there are times when *we* need to step out of the way and let God use us to channel His grace."

❄

In her beautiful book *Box of Butterflies: Discovering the Unexpected Blessings All Around*, Roma said something I hadn't caught when she told me the story in person.

"As I hung up the phone that evening, I prayed, thanking God both for using me and for Della, who, as always, possessed the wisdom I desperately needed.

"Who was I to say God wasn't using me in that moment? How many other times had I limited Him and not been available to be a light to someone who needed it?"

REFLECTIONS

Roma went to the hospital that day to help uplift others, but as a bonus, she received a great gift herself: greater clarity about her job for God—her purpose.

God calls each of us to be His ambassador, an angel on Earth, or, as we often say, a Godwink Link—the unwitting courier of a Godwink to someone else.

Perhaps your role as a real-life angel is the same as Roma's that day in the hospital: to simply pray with someone in need.

Is there someone God wants you to reach out to today, as His angel agent on Earth, with a message of love and hope?

Let your light shine before others,
that they may see your good deeds
and glorify your Father in heaven.
—MATTHEW 5:16 (NIV)

10

Holly and Holly: An Unexpected Friendship

Holly Short was approaching Christmas with cautious optimism. Two years ago she had been hospitalized with depression, and last year her husband, Rick, had been in rehab for alcoholism and depression. Rick had committed himself to sobriety over the holidays—and now, this Christmas, he'd be one year sober. What great news!

She wondered what she could do to celebrate. It should be something special to underscore his achievement.

Then an idea hit her. The local radio station Froggy 97 in Watertown, New York, just ten miles north, always played songs for people on their birthdays and anniversaries. Why not see if they would dedicate Rick's favorite song to him, Kenny Chesney singing "That's Why I'm Here"? He'd love that!

With a slight twinge of nervousness Holly located the number and dialed the phone.

"Froggy 97, this is Cricket," said the cheery voice.

Somewhat surprised that one of the top DJs would be answering the phone herself, Holly said, "Oh . . . Cricket . . . I was calling to see if I could get a song dedicated to my husband, who's one year sober." She told her the artist and song.

"Can you hold, please? Let me be sure we have that song."

Moments later Cricket was back on the line. "Yes! We can do it."

Holly thanked her.

"What's your name, and where do you live?" asked Cricket.

"My name is Holly, and I'm from Adams Center."

There was a momentary silence. Then Cricket giggled. "*My* name is Holly. And *I'm* from Adams Center!" She added, "Cricket's my DJ name."

"Oh, my goodness, that's amazing!" said Holly Short.

She was so flabbergasted she never asked another question, such as "Where in Adams Center do you live?" She just hung up the phone and stared at the goose bumps popping up on her arms.

❄

The following Sunday morning, Holly and Rick went to church at the Adams Center Baptist Church at the top of Wilson Lane, one block from their home.

The pastor invited people to share their joys and concerns and began by announcing that there was a celebrity among them that morning. He looked past Holly and Rick to a pew farther back, and said, "Visiting us this morning is a well-known DJ at Froggy 97. You know her as 'Cricket.' Her real name is Holly Gaskin."

As soon as Holly Short heard the pastor say "celebrity," she'd sensed that he was going to mention "Cricket's" name, but she was so astonished that she sat there motionless.

After the service Holly Gaskin approached Holly Short. "Are you Holly?" she asked. Holly Short nodded.

"I had that feeling. When you called the other day, I got goose bumps," continued Holly Gaskin.

"Me too," said Holly Short softly.

She laughed. "I don't know why, but I was certain I'd see you in church! And this is the first time I've set foot in a church in quite a while."

They chatted for a few minutes, then parted ways.

Holly Short realized that, once again, she had never asked Holly Gaskin where she and her husband lived. But as Holly and Rick passed through the front door of the church, they could see that the other Holly and her husband were going down Wilson Lane. Right past their own house!

When the other couple got to the corner of North Street, they turned right. Then Holly and Rick watched them go into the second house on the right. Holly Short got goose bumps again. That meant that her side lawn fence was the backyard fence of Holly Gaskin!

Wow! What are the odds that two strangers named Holly, living in the same small village, have houses that abut each other?

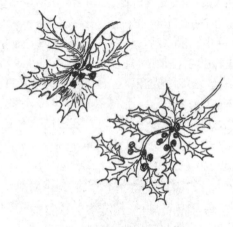

*

After that day, the two Hollys got to know each other and discovered that they had plenty of things in common. They learned that both of them had suffered from depression, both of their husbands struggled with alcoholism, both of them wrote music, and both of them loved cats.

Both of them have now moved away from Adams Center, but they reflect warmly on that Christmas. "Holly was a gift of friendship that year," says Holly Short. "And the following year we invited her to join us for Christmas dinner."

"We were brought together for a reason," observes Holly Gaskin, adding, "We sure have a lot of Godwinks!"

※

There's one more very Godwinky aspect to this story. It's best described by what I wrote to each of the Hollys.

"When you left the church, went down Wilson Lane, and turned right onto North Street," I said, "if you had walked the distance of just two more houses, to the corner of Teeple Street, then looked left, you'd have been gazing at the house that *I* was born and raised in."

Both Hollys said they got goose bumps again.

Me too.

Even now, as I read this, I say, "Wow . . . what are the odds?"

REFLECTIONS

God ordains the times and places where we should live. He knew that the two Hollys needed to encourage each other, and so He divinely aligned their lives to connect.

God cares about every detail of your life. He cares about your finances, your health, your marriage, your local church, and your neighbors.

Isn't it comforting to know that God cares so much about you that He knows where you live?

> *In all your ways acknowledge him,*
> *and he shall direct your paths.*
>
> —Proverbs 3:5–6 (KJV)

11

Candy: The Story of Her Story

Wending through traffic, Candy Chand glanced at her watch. Christmas was days away, and the stresses of the season were making her shoulders ache. Furrowing her brow, she reviewed her list of to-dos. Was she mistaken, or was she adding more than subtracting?

The priority of the moment: getting to Nicholas's school on time. The first- through sixth-graders were having a dress rehearsal for the so-called "winter pageant."

"Why don't they call it what it is?" she said out loud as she drove.

Her mind moved to a more harmonious thought: *Thank God Nicholas has no problem with my night schedule at the hospital.* It was a blessing that at six he was oblivious to his mommy's coming to dress rehearsal rather than the real performance that evening.

"No prima donna there." She smiled. Nicholas was a no-stress kid. But the very mention of "stress" took her mind back to her earlier thoughts.

"Winter pageant? Don't get me started," she said, shaking her head in quick little movements as she searched through the windshield, confirming that again none of the stores displayed the word *Christmas*.

Christ is rejected, and so am I, she thought. *How many publisher rejections do I now have?*

She'd lost count. It was small comfort to have the nicest stack of turn-downs: "A fourth-grade girl's diary is a good idea, but . . ." "Your children's book, *Nikki Lamar's Private Diary*, has compelling characters and dialogue, but . . ."

Just how many turn-downs should it take to get someone to give it up?

Sometimes she wondered whether the cancer patients at the hospital were teaching her a lesson she should learn. Some had confided that there was a peace in accepting the inevitable.

Wouldn't my life be less stressful if I accepted the inevitable and stopped fighting a fruitless battle?

At that moment she was reminded of her mother's encouraging words: "You're going to be a writer when you grow up, Candy. Believe that with all your heart." Her mom saw her fulfilling her dream.

Oh, how I wish I could pick up the phone and call Mom, she thought. But sadly, her mom had passed away.

Would her mother be disappointed if she caught her even *thinking* of giving up?

In that instant, arriving at the school parking lot was a relief. It meant she could avoid dealing with her mother's prodding all the way from Heaven.

Candy expelled a quiet sigh. Another small miracle. She'd gotten there on time.

A few other parents, teachers, and other children had gathered in the lunchroom performance area to see what this year's Christmas pageant would bring.

There, I've said *it*, Candy thought defiantly. "*Christmas* pageant!"

The music teacher was herding her youngsters like little sheep into position for the dress rehearsal of their big number. *How cute can little kids be?* Candy mused as an involuntary smile swept over her face.

As they began, Candy drew in a breath. She realized they were about to perform a song called "Christmas Love." Her appreciation for Nicholas's teacher and the school instantly soared.

Imagine that! A school that is using the actual word for the holiday we're celebrating!

She was proud of them for doing what is right.

But in the course of the next few minutes, Candy was

totally unprepared for the life-changing Godwink that was about to happen. As the adorable flock of children commenced their performance, adorned in red scarves and fuzzy white mittens, something unexpected altered the map of Candy's journey as a writer.

※

"In that moment, I instantly knew that God was sending me a message," she reflected later. "It was a clear sign that putting aside my quest to write was not an option. God was not only making the decision, but—through a charming Godwink—He was providing the story He wanted told."

A heartwarming story called *Christmas Love* poured out onto Candy's computer screen that evening at home. She decided to test the story by posting it on the internet. Within hours it was shared by tens of thousands of people around the globe.

She described what happened when the teacher directed each of the five-year-olds to lift up a placard with a letter from the alphabet, thereby spelling out the name of the song, "Christmas Love."

The performance was going smoothly, until suddenly we noticed her—a small, quiet girl in the front row holding the letter "M" upside down—totally unaware her letter "M" appeared as a "W."

The audience of first- through sixth-graders snickered at this little one's mistake. But she had no idea they were laughing at her, so she stood tall, proudly holding her "W."

Although many teachers tried to shush the children, the laughter continued until the last letter was raised, and we all saw it together. A hush came over the audience, and eyes began to widen.

In that instant, we understood—the reason we were there, why we celebrated the holiday in the first place, why even in the chaos there was a purpose for our festivities. For when the last letter was held high, the message could be read loud and clear: CHRIST WAS LOVE.

And I believe He still is.

This story, previously featured in *When God Winks at You,* fulfilled Candy's mother's prophecy for her to become a writer.

Christmas Love is now the title of one of seven books Candy has had published. With more to come!

REFLECTIONS

Candy Chand's experience was a wink and a nod from God to hang in there. He was not about to let her give up her aims to become a writer.

In the midst of the hustle-bustle, God showed up with a perfect gift of encouragement. Through a Godwink, He pointed to an open door for her to pursue the desires of her heart.

That sweet Christmas Godwink put everything into perspective.

Do you ever feel that the more you try to control the pandemonium in your life, the more you realize you can't?

If He did that for Candy, He'll do it for you.

Commit your way to the LORD;
trust in him and he will do this.

—Psalms 37:5 (NIV)

12

Dan: Christmas History on Capitol Hill

Dan Cummins ran a hand through his dark hair and leaned back in the chair. He loved studying American history as much as digging through family genealogy. He found that both hobbies unearthed fascinating discoveries of the past.

But what he had just read bolted him upright.

He pensively gazed through the window of his East Texas home, reiterating in his mind the words of historian David Barton: "Three weeks before Christmas, on December 4, 1800, Congress approved the use of the Capitol Building as a church building."

As a church building? Dan repeated to himself.

He began jotting down notes to be sure to remember.

- From Thomas Jefferson through Abraham Lincoln, many presidents attended church at the Capitol, often with two thousand people in attendance.

- From 1800 to 1857, church services were held in various locations in the Capitol Building.
- Then, from 1857 to 1869, they were held in the newly built House Chamber.

His interest was further piqued by the next revelation:

- In fact, the first official use of the building we know today as the House Chamber was a church service on December 13, 1857.

"It's amazing so few people know that!" he said aloud.

Dan was himself the pastor of the tiny storefront Bridlewood Church in the town of Bullard, Texas, and various questions swooped into his mind: *If church services were held in the Capitol Building for sixty-nine years—why did they stop?*

Then, as the next question began to form in his mind, he wanted to savor it, letting it unfurl like an American flag: *If regular church services existed once, could they exist again in the Capitol Building?*

❄

Dan couldn't wait to share what was incubating in his mind with JoAnn, his wife and partner in everything.

"JoAnn, do you have a minute?" he asked.

With a look of curiosity, she sat down next to her husband.

"Honey, this could be a God idea." He smiled. "A *big* God idea!"

She tilted her head ever so slightly. She'd been down this path before. His earnestness was familiar.

"Think about all the unbelievable things God has done to shift us from pastoring a little church here in Texas to praying with opinion leaders in Washington."

In a counting motion he touched one forefinger to the other. "Eight years ago, in 2008, God placed it on our hearts to pray with our tiny congregation 'to open a door for our church to be a blessing to the nation.' Right?"

JoAnn nodded.

"After that, we've literally watched God 'open the door.' "

JoAnn watched as her husband successively counted off on his other fingers. "He led us to amazing connections, renewed friendships, and then, through our congressman, we were given access to Speaker John Boehner, who gave us permission to use Statuary Hall in the Capitol Building for the *Washington: A Man of Prayer* event. Who could have predicted that you and I would be organizing the annual event honoring our first president, for three years running?"

JoAnn nodded several times, raising her eyebrows in agreement. Then she asked, "So . . . what's the big God idea?"

Fueled with fresh enthusiasm, Dan looked into her eyes and spoke deliberately. "How would you feel if what God is *really* opening the door to—for us to be a blessing to our nation—is that we are to hold regular *weekly church services* in the Capitol Building?"

JoAnn knew her husband well. He believed in the nudges from God and the power of prayer, just as she did.

"Let's pray and talk about it," she said.

For the next hour they prayed and talked. She asked thoughtful questions, and Dan reviewed what he had discovered in his research: that the Capitol Building had been approved as a church building in 1800; that church services had been held there for 69 years; that for some unknown reason they had stopped; and that for the last 144 years, there had been no regular church services there, as far as anyone knew.

"Wouldn't it be exciting to start them up again?" asked Dan, wide-eyed, with kidlike delight.

They both smiled.

"Let's go to lunch. We'll celebrate," she said, jumping up from her chair.

❋

Dan's "big God idea"—to try to resume weekly church services in the Capitol Building—led to many conversations with others. First, he wanted to try to tie up loose ends in the historical perspective. He was unable to find information in various historians' work as to why the church services had been halted in 1869, and no historian he consulted knew of any other regular church services that had been held there during the intervening 144 years.

Assessing that his and JoAnn's three years in and out of Washington had given them a unique opportunity to earn the trust of the Speaker of the House and others with whom they had worked to produce the *Washington: A Man of Prayer* event, Dan then sought the support of several congressmen. They agreed to join Dan and JoAnn in seeking permission to use a meeting room somewhere in the Capitol Building for Wednesday-evening church services.

When word came down that Speaker Boehner would assign them a room to use, Dan and JoAnn were exuberant! That was in August 2014.

Shortly thereafter, their small church in Texas graciously relieved them from their pastoral duties and sent them on their way, wrapped in the prayers of a loving congregation.

About the same time, Dan sparked a relationship with a magnificent, spirit-filled singer named Steve Amerson, known as "America's Tenor," and invited him to join forces with them as their worship pastor.

❋

In his spare time, whenever Dan wasn't preparing for a Sunday sermon or walking the halls of Congress, he pursued his hobby of tracing his family's history. But his quest to map the Cummins genealogy had gotten stuck. He had been able to follow the branches of the family tree back to the small community of Cynthiana in Paris County, Kentucky, but that's where the trail had ended, leaving him somewhat frustrated.

Yet in ways he could never have imagined, Dan was about to be divinely aligned from one Godwink to another, taking him to where God wanted him to go.

❋

Dan was at the Capitol Building, preparing for the launch of the rebirth of church services on Capitol Hill; JoAnn was in Texas, wrapping up the sale of their home and getting ready to move their furnishings.

Dan was feeling the stress. It seemed as though a hundred details were falling through the cracks.

It was about 11 p.m. when he walked outside and sat down on the edge of a fountain on the East Capitol Plaza, under the moon. He looked up at the beauty of the lighted dome of the Capitol and then at the moon, and he prayed.

He prayed for clarity and strength. He asked for certainty where little certainty appeared to exist.

At that moment a scripture popped into his mind that seemed to confirm the God nudging that they had been following—for God to "open a door." A verse from Revelation came back to him. It was "I have placed before you an open door that no one can shut."

A peace instantly came over Dan that he couldn't explain. *Why didn't I think of that scripture before?*

He lifted his gaze back up to the moon, now hanging like a painted picture over the dome of the Capitol.

Speaking aloud in a grateful voice, he said, "Thank you, God. That's just what I needed: Your assurances that this is *the* door that *You* have opened and that *You* will give us strength that we don't have on our own to walk through it."

The next day the event went well—beyond expectations.

He later picked up his Bible and reread the full scripture from Revelation 3:8:

> *I know your deeds. See, I have placed before you an open door that no one can shut. I know that you have little strength, yet you have kept my word and have not denied my name.*
>
> —REVELATION 3:8 (NIV)

❄

Soon the Wednesday-night church services were catching on and going well. As Pastor Dan and Steve Amerson walked the corridors of the Capitol, more and more members of Congress greeted them warmly.

Something pressed upon Dan to review his research on the history of church services in the Capitol Building. He returned to the historian David Barton's website. He was suddenly jolted by seeing something he had somehow overlooked the first time: the name of the preacher who had conducted the first church service in the newly christened House Chamber on December 13, 1857.

In a flash Dan knew that it was an astounding Godwink!

The pastor's name, the rector of the local Trinity Church, was Bishop George David Cummins. That's right, Cummins—spelled the same as Dan's last name!

Dan's family had always known that their name—Cummins without the *g*—was highly unusual. The first pastor to preach in the new House Chamber had the *same* name?

Really? he thought. *How could I have missed this the first time I researched it?*

Could it be that they were relatives?

"JoAnn, you're not going to believe this!" he shouted.

Dan began an immediate search of the genealogy records of Bishop George David Cummins. He followed the trail. He got excited when it took him to the very same community in Paris County, Kentucky, where his previous search had gotten stuck: Cynthiana. But there was no record connecting the dots; no evidence that he and pastor Bishop Cummins were actually related.

Dan phoned a friend in Baltimore who was also a genealogy buff, Joe d'Entremont. He thought perhaps Joe could help.

A week or two later Joe and his wife, Peggy, visited Dan and JoAnn in DC. He handed Dan a package.

Having done his own research into the bishop's lineage, Joe had discovered the existence of a memoir written by Bishop Cummins's wife and had purchased it for Dan. "I haven't looked at this," he said, "but maybe you'll find some clues."

Dan was thrilled. He couldn't wait to read it.

❋

Later, with the memoir in his lap, Dan gingerly turned the pages. It excited him to read the name at the top of the first page: Rev. George David Cummins.

His heart beat faster, thinking that somehow, all of these events—his quest to find his family lineage and his and JoAnn's new journey to be "a blessing for our nation"—were somehow tethered by God's winks and designs.

Dan turned to the first entry that the bishop's wife said her husband had written into his prayer journal. It caused him to expel a quick, involuntary gasp of air. Bishop Cummins's first words in his prayer journal were "I have placed before you an open door that no one can shut."

Wow! thought Dan.

A century and a half earlier, that preacher had quoted the same words in the Bible, Revelation 3:8, that had guided Dan and JoAnn in their journey from Bullard, Texas, to Washington, DC.

"JoAnn, you've got to see this!" he shouted excitedly. "God is in this, right in the middle of it!"

❋

A few weeks later Dan was honored to receive a request from Father Patrick Conroy, the chaplain of the House of Representatives, asking him to present the prayer at the opening of a session of the House. Dan looked at the date written on the paper when he would speak: December 13, 2016. He was quietly shocked.

No one on Earth can possibly know what I know at this moment, he said to himself. *I'm in the middle of God's tapestry, watching Him weave my life as He reveals yet another extraordinary Godwink.*

December 13 was the exact anniversary of the day that Bishop George David Cummins had dedicated and preached the first of his many sermons in the House Chamber!

Now, exactly 159 years later, another pastor by the name of Cummins—the very person whom God had divinely aligned to resume weekly church services in the Capitol Building—had been chosen by God to open the session of the House of Representatives from the same podium.

God, there's no way we can compute the odds of that! thought Dan.

His only wish at that moment was that he'd been able to establish that he and Bishop Cummins were indeed relatives.

❄

On Facebook the morning of December 13, Dan decided to tell folks about the significance of the day. He had an inspired thought: *I wonder if I could find a photo of Bishop George David Cummins. At least I could post our two photos.*

He found one. If ever there was a doubt that God had divinely aligned two relatives named Cummins to do His work under the Capitol Dome, there was the evidence. They look nearly identical!

❄

In 2014, Dan and JoAnn Cummins began their Wednesday-evening services, now known as Capitol Worship, and later added Sunday-morning services specifically for Capitol staff and the Capitol Police. Their outreach on the Hill and with members of Congress on both sides of the aisle continues to grow.

❄

In December 2017, Dan, JoAnn, and Steve Amerson achieved one more milestone in the Capitol Building: they inaugurated Carols in the Capitol, which they expect to be an annual event. It's a Christmas carol sing-along under Steve's musical direction in Statuary Hall of the United States Capitol.

Seats set up under the majestic Capitol Dome were filled to the maximum as members of Congress and their families felt the joyous music of the season reverberate through the chamber.

Louise and I were honored to join Senate chaplain Barry Black and Father Conroy of the House of Representatives as speakers.

REFLECTIONS
Faith is not a feeling but a divine gift from God.

Faith is taking God at His word and obeying His

commands even though your life is a series of twists and turns.

Just like Dan Cummins, you can't see around the bends in your road, but God can. And just as Dan took solace in the time-tested words of the ancient scriptures, so can you.

> *Faith is the substance of things hoped for,*
> *the evidence of things not seen.*
> —HEBREWS 11:1 (KJV)

The Bible is filled with stories of people who also couldn't see evidence of what was coming around the bend but maintained their faith in what they hoped for.

God told Noah to build an ark because there was going to be a massive flood. He did. Abraham's wife, Sarah, was way beyond childbearing years, but God told her she would conceive a son. She did.

What God had placed on their hearts seemed to defy all human logic, but those leaders of the Bible took God at His word and had faith in the unseen.

Your life may seem like the jumbled pieces of a jig-saw puzzle spread over the dining room table. You may wonder what God is up to. But think about the real-life, contemporary faith that Dan and JoAnn were called upon to hope for—to pull up stakes in Texas and move to Washington, DC, to do something that hadn't been done in 144 years—and how they subsequently discovered the "evidence of things not seen."

When you open your gift of faith, you'll see that God has fit every single piece of your life together perfectly. In fact, He has created a masterpiece!

> *We are God's masterpiece.*
> *He has created us anew*
> *in Christ Jesus, so we can do*
> *the good things he planned for us long ago.*
> —EPHESIANS 2:10 (NLT)

13

Louise and Spotty:
A Will and a Way

I was one of those "dorky" kids who wore saddle shoes. I was not what you'd call a social butterfly. As a matter of fact, I was painfully shy. I loved animals and felt more comfortable around my four-legged friends than the human race.

Every December, without fail, I would meticulously write out my Christmas list of presents that I wanted. At the top of the list were three big letters: DOG.

I so much wanted to have my own dog to play with and take care of. That wish was never granted. Every year my mother would emphatically say "NO!" and that was the end of the discussion until the next year.

I used to dream that I would wake up on Christmas morning and find a furry little puppy under the tree. I prayed so hard, but it wasn't meant to be.

I certainly understood why God didn't answer my prayer, but it still hurt and it didn't quench my desire to love a puppy.

My mother's dislike for dogs—really a fear—began when she was a little girl. Her beloved grandfather had tragically died after being bitten by a rabid dog. He had suffered a horrible death. That had left my mother devastated and gripped with fear every time she saw a dog.

One day I made the mistake of asking one more time. She was having an extremely stressful day. Her nerves were frayed, and on top of that she was dealing with a migraine headache. She suddenly blurted out, "The *only* way you are going to get a dog is if somebody leaves it to you in their will!"

Gulp. I felt a lump in my throat as I held back tears. I never asked her again.

God did give me a partial answer to my prayer, though.

Our former tenant Bill Stellberger had an elderly mother who needed a dog sitter. Even though I was only twelve years old, he knew I would be the perfect person to fill that bill.

Mrs. Stellberger had the smartest and most wonderful dog named Spotty. She was a mix of cocker spaniel and border collie. We hit it off immediately, and it was love at first sight for both of us.

Every time I would step foot in Mrs. Stellberger's house, Spotty would leap into my arms and lick my face, crying with delight at seeing me. I cherished the time we spent together and felt such sadness when I had to leave. I counted the days when I would see her again.

One day just before Christmas, Bill knocked on the door and told us the sad news that his mother had passed away. He then disclosed that his mother had left me something in her will.

Me? Why me? I wondered. I wasn't a member of the family.

"I need to get it. It's in the car," he said, turning from the doorway.

Mom and I watched as Bill went to his car and opened the door. Spotty jumped out and made a beeline for me! She wrapped her forelegs around me and could hardly contain herself.

With tears in my eyes I thanked Bill profusely, but I knew my mother's stand on dogs. I was frozen in time and didn't want the love fest to end.

Out of the corner of my eye I looked up at Mom. She had a blank look on her face.

Does she remember what she once said—the only way I'll get a dog is if it's in somebody's will? What if she doesn't remember . . . and says no? Will I ever see Spotty again? If I don't, it would be devastating.

I tentatively looked up at her, my voice shaking, mustering the courage to whisper, "Ma . . . can I keep her?"

She didn't answer.

I could feel the tears welling up and my face flushing.

It seemed like a lifetime. Her strained response finally came. "Yeah. I guess I don't have much of a choice!"

I never felt such joy. I couldn't stop crying happy

tears. Spotty was mine! *Mine!* God had given her to me! My life was complete!

Every day I spent with my precious friend was pure joy. She would wait for me, looking out the front window, tail wagging, anticipating my return from school. We were inseparable. I never felt such unconditional love. (Not until I met SQuire, of course!)

My mother eventually fell in "like" with Spotty, and her fear of dogs disappeared. God gave me the desire of my heart and answered my prayer in the most unexpected way.

Spotty lived to be seventeen. She was my best friend and my confidante. When the dreaded time came that we had to "put her to sleep," it was the saddest day of my life.

To this moment I can't think about my sweet Spotty without tearing up. I know in my heart that I will see her again. I can picture her now, waiting for me at Heaven's gate—as she did in the front window of our old house—tail wagging and ready to jump into my arms again.

Until then, SQuire will have to do!

✻

Of course, I'm being facetious about SQuire, but those of you who have pets know that some of the greatest gifts and deepest joys that God gives us come in furry packages. Spotty wasn't a gift that came in a box. But as Mom and I stood on the doorstep that day, Spotty sure became my best Christmas gift ever!

REFLECTIONS

Was there ever something that you wanted more than anything, and you prayed for it but knew there was no earthly way that God could possibly answer your prayer? Don't lose faith. God can do anything.

He can move Heaven and Earth just for you. And, mindful of the old adage "Where there's a will there's a way," He'll make a way where there *is* no way.

God will also answer your prayers with Godwinks, maybe just not the way you expect.

Who knows, perhaps you'll get a Christmas Godwink like mine . . . it's a gift of friendship that comes with snuggles and a lick on the face!

Yvonne, Part I: The Spirit of Christmas Every Day

The year was 1978.

As Yvonne began her talk, she looked around the room at her audience: mostly men, some women.

"There's been much focus on helping *children* with special needs," she said firmly. "Rightly so—but we are only children for one-quarter of our lives and we're *adults* for the other three-quarters. In our society we simply don't know what to do with adults with disabilities."[1]

Yvonne Streit, herself the mother of a child with disabilities and the founder of the Briarwood School for children with learning disabilities, was making another speech to a Rotary Club. For two years she'd been speaking before any service club, church, or organization that would let her in the door. She never failed to tell her listeners that God is the founder of her organization and that she just works for Him.

Her aim, month after month, was to raise money to

study the development of a facility called the Brookwood Community, which would address the needs of the population of learning-disabled people over eighteen.

"This is where we need your help," she finished strongly with a direct, action step. "We need the funds to visit top facilities for adults with disabilities—in both America and Europe—in order to learn what they've learned, then apply it here."

At the end of her speech, some of the attendees smiled, nodded, or said "Nice job." Most just left.

※

"One more speech with no takers," she disappointedly told her husband, Dave, that evening.

With an exasperated look, she shook her head slowly.

"In my prayers I really thought God was telling us to *GO* with our dream. Evidently I misinterpreted Him. I'm ready to throw in the towel."

At bedtime she continued pondering her predicament. "Did I misunderstand You, God?"

In her heart she acknowledged that we sometimes *tell God* where we want Him to go, instead of *asking Him* where He wants us to go. It's when we choose the latter that we're more likely to receive His supernatural confirmations.

Godwinks.

The next day at 8:30 a.m., the phone rang. It was Frank, a man who had heard Yvonne speak at the Rotary luncheon the day before.

"I'd like to come by and give you something," he said.

Frank arrived at Yvonne's office at 9:00 a.m. and handed her a check for $10,000, adding, "This is to study the idea for Brookwood."

"I was flabbergasted," said Yvonne.

At 9:30 a.m. Yvonne's assistant director gleefully shared more good news: "A man who heard you speak at Rotary telephoned. He's sending over a check for $7,500!"

At 10:00 a.m., St. Luke's United Methodist Church phoned. "We're sending you a check for $25,000 to study the Brookwood idea."

At 11:00 a.m. another call came in, this one from the Barrow Foundation. "We'd like to contribute $30,000 for your study."

WOW!

All she could say was, "Thank You, Father! We *didn't* misunderstand Your message. You've now made it abundantly clear—this is a *GO!*"

In truth, Yvonne never did lose her faith. She was just momentarily lamenting her situation. In fact, as she looked back, she realized that her faith actually grew while waiting upon God to answer her prayers.

As Yvonne moved through the process of asking for His guidance and following His nudges to persistently seek funding for Brookwood, He was stretching her faith and teaching her to lean on Him in every situation.

God then turned on the spigot, and out came a gusher

of Godwinks: a total of $72,500 in contributions, all in the space of two hours in a single morning!

Today, over three decades later, the Brookwood Community sits on one corner of 485 acres west of Houston, near Katy, Texas. It serves as a model for hundreds of other organizations in this field. People come from around the world to attend Brookwood's Center for Learning to study why it's so successful in helping their "citizens develop self-respect and self-reliance by providing purpose."

"Citizen" is the term Brookwood uses to describe the 112 residents and 115 daytime individuals who live and work at the community.

About five years ago our then-twenty-seven-year-old son, Grant, who suffered from a brain injury at birth, was accepted at Brookwood Community. Grant has thrived there and enjoys his work in horticulture.

Each year on the first weekend of December, hundreds of people travel from miles around Houston for Brookwood's biggest annual event, their Christmas Open House. The highlight is a delightful show performed by the citizens, as well as the famed Brookwood Citizen Hand Bell Choir, which at multiple times of the year performs for various churches and other organizations.

Visitors to the Christmas event have learned to telephone well in advance to reserve a table at the Brookwood Café in order to enjoy fine dining under the guidance of a Culinary Institute of America chef. The waitstaff, consisting of Brookwood teachers and citizens who have specially designed notepads, with visually cued symbols, cheerfully take your order.

Before or after lunch, visitors can browse through the elegant Brookwood Gift Shop with items that could easily grace the pages of *Better Homes and Gardens* and purchase professional-looking crafts made by the hands of citizens. On display is beautiful pottery, Brookwood chocolates, Shudde Brothers western hats, and other decor items created on the premises.

Houstonians can also purchase horticulture items from the 300,000 plants propagated and planted by the citizens each year, not including 48,000 Christmas poinsettias, one of the state's largest annual crops.[2]

When one of the citizens was complimented on the beautiful plants he was planting, he said, "That is because God has His hand over my hand to help me."

According to Yvonne Streit, "That kind of acknowledgment has become the heart and soul on which Brookwood is built—how the citizens can actually *do* what they didn't *think* they could do."

The income derived from the enterprises and products produced by the citizens of Brookwood—remarkably about $6 million a year—helps to sustain their community.

✳

You're invited to visit the Brookwood Community any time of year. But if you're in the Houston area on the first weekend of December, be sure to visit Brookwood's Christmas Open House. It's really quite special and a wonderful "spiritual jump-start" to the Christmas season.

You'll discover why the citizens who live at Brookwood spread the Spirit of Christmas every day of the year.

REFLECTIONS

Often our prayers are not answered right away, nor in the manner we expect. But when God decides to open the gates for Godwinks, He'll frequently do it with a flourish. Almost like He's showing off for you—letting you know He heard your prayers.

To confirm His presence, He sometimes creates the

cause-and-effect that became evident to Yvonne; fervent prayers resulted in a series of astonishing Godwinks.

❋

In the next story, you'll see another insight into the history of the Brookwood Community and the personality of its extraordinary founder, Yvonne Streit.

If you like surprises, you'll love this story.

15

Yvonne, Part II: The Rest of the Surprising Story

Not long ago, Yvonne Streit finally gave in to the coaxing of many of her supporters, including us, and memorialized the extraordinary story of the Brookwood Community, which she founded, in a wonderful book called *Everybody's Got a Seed to Sow: The Brookwood Story.*

She said that she would attempt to write the book only with this caveat: "It must be a book about God's leadership of our dedicated staff—many of whom have been here twenty to twenty-five years—as well as the amazing citizens and the donors who give of their time, guidance, gifts, and service."

In the book she describes Brookwood as "a God-centered educational community for adults with special needs; providing them with purpose, meaningful work, and a fulfilling life."

She is also quick to tell you that "because we don't accept one nickel of government money, proceeds from the sale of the book will go to the citizens of Brookwood and to its outreach programs."

※

One of our favorite stories in Yvonne's book occurred in the early development of the Briarwood School, the predecessor of Brookwood. It is about a particularly difficult youngster named Tracy who attended the school when it was located in a church.[1] He was an eight-year-old boy who had been kicked out of every school he had attended.

She described him as "a young man who used daredevil tactics as an attention-getting device." He ran out in front of cars to scare the drivers. And more than once, he climbed up onto the roof of the one-story church.

One day Yvonne was told that Tracy was on the roof again and had refused to come down.

"I went out and asked him to come down but, as expected, he refused," says Yvonne. After considerable conversation, he said, "Okay, I'll come down, but when I do I'm going to stab you in the 'laig.'"

In Texas, she explains, "laig" means "leg."

As promised, as soon as Tracy came down off the roof, he picked up a stick and stabbed her in the "laig."

"Not badly," she says with a laugh, "but he did, and then he lay down on the grass and refused to get up."

Yvonne looked at the boy and said firmly, "Tracy, I

don't care what you do, you are not getting kicked out of this school—and that's that!"

He looked up from the grass and said, "But . . . I stabbed you, Mrs. Streit."

"I know that, and I don't care. You are a very smart boy who is confused about a lot of things right now. But that will not stop you from being a really good man and doing really good things, which I know you are capable of!"

That moment was a turning point for Tracy.

It didn't happen overnight, but over time he began to make an effort, did his work, and even surprised himself with his accomplishments.

Some two decades later, Tracy called Yvonne and told her that he was going to be in Houston and he'd like to visit. He said, "I want to come because y'all saved my life."

He did come and was a great inspiration to the students at Briarwood and the citizens and staff of the Brookwood Community. Having achieved considerable success in his field of endeavor, Tracy told Yvonne that he'd like to provide a scholarship for "a kid just like me." She laughed and said, "Tracy, I don't think there is another kid just like you."

❋

Tracy's life had made a dramatic U-turn because someone had believed in him when he didn't believe in himself. Yvonne knew he had untapped talents, but who would have thought that that ornery kid named Woodrow Tracy Harrelson would turn out to be a famous award-winning actor known as Woody Harrelson?

Can we say it together? Wow—what a Godwink!

REFLECTIONS

On a personal note, as the parents of a special-needs child, we prayed for our son to be in a safe, supportive environment where he could grow and thrive.

As a dad, when I walk around the Brookwood campus observing my son and the other citizens joyfully working and playing, I am so thankful for that answered prayer.

Woody Harrelson would tell you never to under-estimate the gift of a smile, a kind word, or a listening ear. The smallest act of caring can turn someone's life around. When you do that—as the staff and teachers at Briarwood and Brookwood do—you leave your "heart-print" on someone's life.

We may indeed learn when we get to Heaven that God has saved the most honored seats at His table for those who spend time on Earth helping those with special needs.

> *Therefore encourage one another*
> *and build each other up,*
> *just as in fact you are doing.*
> —1 THESSALONIANS 5:11 (NIV)

16

Sonja: Secret Santas

These were the darkest moments of Sonja's life. She had hoped, desperately, that her divorce from an abusive marriage would finally lift her from fear and stress. Yet she never anticipated that the aftermath could be just as bad.

The nine years of coparenting after her divorce had been a constant struggle as her ex-husband attempted to manipulate the children against her. Eventually there had been a court battle that had racked up legal fees she couldn't afford.

Now, with the two oldest kids off on their own, her husband had mounted a campaign to convince her youngest daughter, a twelve-year-old, to come live with him. Unfortunately, her daughter's consent to do so persuaded the court. Sonja was devastated.

The debris lying in the wake of her struggle was both emotional and financial. Her heart was so wounded she thought it could never be healed. And with Christmas coming, she had no idea how she was going to buy presents for the kids.

Her salary as a dental hygienist was barely enough to make ends meet. On top of that, with the court's ruling that her daughter would live with her father, Sonja was now required to pay child support.

She decided to take bold measures. In order to move closer to her job, thereby reducing travel costs, she put her house up for rent, located thirty miles outside Beaumont, Texas. She prayed that she could then find a place in the city at a reasonable rent.

After months of feeling emotionally pummeled, two Godwinks gave her a flicker of hope. First, she found the perfect apartment that was rent free for the first month! A day or so later, one of her dental patients, Melanie Bieber, the owner of the upscale women's boutique Pappagallo in Beaumont, offered her a part-time job during the Christmas holidays.

That was another answered prayer, Godwink number two. *Wow. Maybe things are turning around!* she thought.

Sonja's second job started immediately. She would work two evenings a week after leaving the dentist's office at 5 p.m. and all day on Saturdays.

She loved Pappagallo. She liked her coworkers and got to know every pretty item in the inventory—jewelry, handbags, clothing—and because she was innately a people person, she enjoyed helping customers.

Sometimes Sonja allowed herself to feel like Cinderella. She could just imagine how certain items would look on her or in her home. Of course, everything was way beyond her means—but she could fantasize how that Brighton bracelet with the matching earrings would look on her or see herself in her kitchen, sipping from that adorable Vera Bradley coffee mug.

Two weeks before Christmas, Melanie Bieber announced that she would be holding a Christmas party at her home the following Saturday evening. All of her employees were invited, about a dozen people in all.

For months Sonja had been carrying so many burdens on her back that she welcomed the festive spirit of a Christmas party. Getting together and having pleasant conversation with others would be a rare joy.

The Pappagallo office manager, Karen, told Sonja that they typically organized a "secret Santa" for the annual Christmas party. The way it worked was that everyone's name would be placed into a bowl, and you'd draw the identity of the person for whom you'd purchase a small gift; something around $20 in value.

Uh-oh, thought Sonja, *that's another expense*. But she had no choice—she would have to do it.

※

The next Saturday, the store closed at 6:30, and Sonja drove the short distance to Melanie's home, a stylish brick colonial in a lovely nearby neighborhood.

After an hour or so of drinks and hors d'oeuvres, mixing and chatting, Melanie asked everyone to find a seat.

Standing next to the Christmas tree, with stacks of brightly wrapped gifts with big red bows behind her, she explained that they were going to play the White Elephant game.

"Normally the game is played with gifts provided by the participants," she said, smiling at the gathering of eager faces. "In this case, however"—she paused for emphasis—"every gift came from Pappagallo."

An audible expression of delight rose from the employees.

"And"—pausing again—"every gift is worth at least two hundred dollars."

A burst of joy erupted from the delighted recipients!

"These are the rules of the game," said Melanie, speaking more loudly to quiet the crowd as one of her helpers passed around a bowl containing slips of white paper. "Everyone draws a number. And that will be the order in which your turn comes up." The guests drew numbers, and then Melanie said, "We'll begin with guest number one."

"That's me!" shouted a lady.

"In a moment you'll come up and select a gift from under the tree," said Melanie.

The lady beamed, looking over and surveying the gifts.

"After you select your gift," continued Melanie, "each person, in order, will have the option of either 'stealing' a gift from someone else or selecting a gift from under the tree."

Directing her comment to the first lady, she said, "If someone 'steals' your gift, *you* get to pick another one from the tree—or steal somebody else's. That's how the game progresses. Pick out a new gift—or steal someone else's."

Waiting for the laughter to subside, she looked around the room. "Everyone got that? One more thing, a gift can only have three owners. The third owner keeps it."

Chatter filled the room as some cracked jokes and others giggled.

Sonja watched as the game progressed toward her number, eight. There was an air of frivolity, and through the babble it was difficult to keep track of who got what.

In fact, from where she was seated, Sonja couldn't even see what some of the presents were.

It came time for her to select a gift. She took one from under the tree. Opening the package carefully, she saw that it was an elegant ceramic teapot. It was nice, but she didn't own it long. The very next person "stole" it from her.

That was repeated on her second turn.

On her third turn, she ended up with a gift that had been twice stolen from someone else: a decorative handbag. A friend who had been seated at the other side of the room walked past just as Sonja was opening her gift.

"Oh, Sonja, you're so lucky. I was the first person who got that. I really wanted that handbag, but it was stolen from me."

Sonja shrugged and said amiably, "I'll trade with you."

"You will?" asked the lady, beaming and thanking her profusely.

The woman went and grabbed a box by her chair, and they traded.

Sonja looked down and lifted the cover of the box. Her mouth fell open. "Oh . . . I don't believe it!" she gasped.

She was holding the Brighton bracelet and matching earrings!

She was speechless. She looked at the woman who had just traded with her. "You got what you wanted . . . and . . . I got what I wanted!"

They both laughed, blinking away the start of tears coming into their eyes.

She hadn't even realized that the White Elephant game had ended. Karen the office manager, who was now handing out the "secret Santa" gifts, placed a small box in Sonja's lap.

She opened it. That time she did cry. It was the Vera Bradley coffee mug.

Looking back, Sonja said, "There's no way those events at the Christmas party were coincidence. They were Godwinks.

"As I left Melanie's home that night, my heart was full of joy. I knew my heavenly Father had shown up to give me the desires of the heart—not so much for the material things, but to show me the love He had for me at the lowest part of my life. It turned out to be one of my most memorable Christmases ever."

REFLECTIONS

Perhaps you can relate to Sonja's situation. Life was tough, as she was going through multiple challenging trials.

God doesn't always free you from difficult times, but He does promise that He will walk through the trials with you.

If you ask Him, as Sonja did, He will give you the gift of peace to bear the burden.

The jewelry and coffee mug that Sonja received were special and personal Godwinks to let her know that He was right there with her. His presence was her present!

Don't let life get you down. Remember the promise He gives us in His Word:

> *I came that they may have and enjoy life,*
> *and have it in abundance.*
>
> —JOHN 10:10 (NIV)

God desires for you to have fun, to laugh and enjoy life to its fullest!

17

Toni and David: An Amazing Christmas Miracle

Toni Espinoza, forty-eight, dark-haired, attractive, the mother of two, looked resolutely into her friend's doubtful eyes, guarding against any more tears.

"That's what I believe, Crawford."

"You've asked God to completely heal David—and to confirm your prayer by making it snow in McAllen, Texas . . . on Christmas Day," Crawford summarized, trying not to mock her.

"Yes."

Crawford was walking a fine line. Toni and Crawford had been close friends all their lives. He needed to respect Toni for confiding in him and seeking his counsel. Yet he also needed to be honest with her.

Gingerly, he continued. "Toni, you've lived here all your life, right?"

She nodded. "Yes."

"Have you ever seen snow?"

She shook her head.

"Do you know that it has not snowed in McAllen, here on the Mexican border, for a hundred and nine years?" He paused a moment for that to sink in, as he looked at her directly. "And never on Christmas?"

"I know, Crawford," said Toni firmly. "But I also know God is going to answer our prayers. My husband is going to live. And God is going to give me a sign—a confirmation."

❋

Over the years, Toni and her husband, David, now forty-nine, had shared many family problems with Crawford and his wife. They had met in grade school, they attended the same church, and their kids played together.

Ever since David had been told by three different cardiologists that he would die within months unless he had a heart transplant, the two families had been in crisis mode. They had discussed the outcome of every doctor's visit, shared medical research, and prayed together.

Now Toni was sharing her confidence with Crawford. Her smile proclaimed the peace in her heart. Her faith that God was going to miraculously save her husband and confirm it with a historic snowfall was unshakable.

Crawford knew better than to argue with her. Once her mind was made up, it was made up. "We're going to pray that your prayers will come true, Toni," he finally said.

❄

Married for thirty years, Toni and David Espinoza lived in a modest home on a quiet street in McAllen, a border city five and a half hours south of Houston. Their two daughters, Trisha and Lisa, were out of the nest and on their way.

Then the devastating news hit them like a ton of bricks.

It was midyear 2004 when David was advised that congestive heart failure had enlarged and damaged his heart to such an extent that it was working at only 10 percent capacity.

"We're surprised he's still walking," said each doctor in so many words.

"A heart transplant is your only option," they told him. "Without it, you have only months to live."

Soon Toni and David were driving up to Houston for further evaluations at the famed DeBakey Heart Center of Baylor Heart Clinic. There it was confirmed that David's ejection fraction—which shows how well the heart pumps with each beat[1]—was only 15 to 20 percent; the normal range is 50 to 70 percent.[2]

DeBakey doctors put David on the list for a heart donor, warning that it often takes nine months or more to find a perfect match. Even if a match was found, the transplant surgery would need to occur within about three hours of finding a donor. The distance from McAllen to Houston, more than a five-hour drive away, was another issue altogether.

Toni and David clung to each other. The doctors' reports made them feel pummeled. Yet what could they do but grasp for strands of hope that they would be delivered a miracle and somehow pull through?

Praying several times a day, Toni cried out to God to save her husband. Yet she became more and more conflicted by the awareness that in order for David to live, someone else would have to die. "That doesn't seem right," she resolved. So instead of a transplant, she asked God for a complete miraculous healing.

❄

By early December, both Toni and David were feeling a tentative peace about their situation, something like a cease-fire in battle.

"I felt we were in God's hands," said David.

"I believed that God had already begun working to heal my husband," said Toni.

Yet she wanted something more, some kind of tangible assurance that God's miracle would be forthcoming.

One day she prayed, "Lord, I know You are healing David. But just to confirm that, could You please make it snow on Christmas Day here in McAllen, Texas?"

She mentioned her prayer to David. When he didn't respond—one of those times when husbands don't seem to register or engage—she decided to tell just three close friends about her pact with God: their close family adviser Crawford Higgins, her sister Sylvia, and her friend Marilyn.

"Snow in McAllen? That's impossible," said her sister.

Marilyn appeared to agree.

Toni just nodded. She wasn't going to argue, yet inwardly she was resolute.

✻

Christmas Eve arrived.

David had the sniffles and knew he needed to set an early alarm for his Santa chores, so he said his goodnights to Toni and the girls and went to bed early. Lisa was not far behind.

Toni and Trisha talked about her work in New York as they occasionally watched Christmas Eve television shows in the background.

At 11:30 p.m., Toni and Trisha decided it was bedtime. Toni cleaned up a few things in the kitchen as Trisha looked through the sliding glass doors into the backyard.

"Mom! Come here. You have to see this!" she shouted.

Toni responded to the urgency in her daughter's voice. She rushed to the sliding doors. Snow flurries were filling the night sky, illuminated by the backyard light.

"Trisha! Is that snow?" She wasn't sure.

"Yes!"

They embraced.

"Your dad's going to be okay," whispered Toni, choking back tears. "Quick, go get Dad and Lisa."

Toni slid open the door to the backyard and stepped onto the lawn, now looking like a fairyland, blanketed with a thin layer of snow. Her rosebushes, in full bloom, were covered in white.

Coatless and alone with God, Toni lifted her face to the heavens, closed her eyes, and inhaled the frosty night air as flecks of snow speckled her hair and stuck to her smiling face.

"Thank You, Lord. Thank You."

The next morning, Christmas Day, bundled-up children burst from their homes all over McAllen, creating first-time snowmen and fanning snow angels on their front lawns.

The local newspaper, *The Monitor*, captured photos for a special edition heralding "Valley gets first good snow since 1895—and its first White Christmas ever."[3]

It was an event that would be talked about for days, yet no one outside of Toni and David's closest friends and family members knew anything about Toni's pact with God.

❋

Four weeks later, Toni and David drove back to Houston for three days of previously scheduled tests at the DeBakey Heart Center. On the third morning, Dr. Guillermo Torre entered the small examining room holding David's chart.

He studied it, checking and rechecking the name at the top. His eyes widened, and his jaw dropped. He looked at the two of them. "I can't explain this," he said with surprise in his voice. "You're not sick anymore!" He again looked at the chart and then at his patient. "David, you're going to be around for a long time."

Tears filled Toni's eyes. David attempted to choke back tears of his own. They stood and hugged each other.

"Thank you, God," she whispered into her husband's ear.

That was an amazing miracle in response to the fervent prayers of one woman who believed that God would not only heal her husband but confirm it with a historic white Christmas.

❄

For anyone who doubts that Toni's sustained prayers were answered with remarkable Godwinks, the medical records from DeBakey Heart Center tell the story.

On David's initial visit, April 27, 2004, doctors wrote, "LV function is severely depressed with LVEF [left ventricle ejection fraction] 15 to 20%." Normal is 50 to 70 percent.

Four weeks after the white Christmas miracle in McAllen, the DeBakey medical report issued on January 24, 2005, states, "Lower limits normal LV function. Qualitative EF is 50%, within the lower range of normal."[4]

Yes . . . it amazingly says "normal."

REFLECTIONS

When we look at the world through man's eyes, we are limited. God wants us to have the faith of a child who believes that God has no limits. When you do, His gifts await you.

In the same manner that you let your earthly father carry your burdens when you were a child, allow God to carry your burdens now. He wants to relieve your stress and give you strength and peace.

> *What is impossible with man*
> *is possible with God.*
>
> —LUKE 18:28 (NIV)

Rhonda: How Chad Came Home for Christmas

Losing a child is a devastating shock for any parent. For Rhonda, losing one of her four beloved boys just before Christmas was heartbreaking.

Tears ran down her cheeks as she sat at the kitchen table studying the photo taken of Chad at his best friend's wedding. He was a handsome twenty-four-year-old in his tuxedo, with a small corsage in his lapel. She gazed at her son's sweet smile and the dimple on his chin; she had always loved the way his dark hair stuck up in the front.

She thought about the day before the funeral, when one of Chad's friends had dropped off his backpack. Her heart was pierced again as she looked inside. She saw the two books he had always carried with him: the Bible and *When God Winks at You*, a small book about God speaking to us through "coincidences."

As she dug deeper into the bag, she found a small card with information about Coca-Cola memorabilia.

She smiled as she thought about how her son had been consumed by his hobby of collecting Coca-Cola items. It had started when he was a little boy and would save up his money to buy the annual Coke Christmas collectible item. He had done that for more than fifteen years. She has a photo of all of Chad's collectibles literally covering the dining room table.

His Coke collection is now carefully packed away, to someday be given to his brothers.

She shook off the thought of Christmas arriving. It was too painful to think about.

⁂

Chad had moved to Arizona with a few of his childhood friends, and without anyone back home realizing it, he had lost his way in life. He had several DUIs, including a traffic accident in which someone had been injured.

That's when Rhonda realized her son needed help for his drinking. She arranged for Chad to come home to Minot, North Dakota, and go through treatment for alcoholism.

A short while later, Chad had to return to Arizona for his court case. No one could believe the outcome. Everyone was stunned. He had been sentenced to prison for seven years!

It was horrible, and it only got worse.

Chad called from prison and said he had suffered beatings. He was in constant fear because others had targeted him for not conforming to the "rules" of prison gang members. He refused to join a gang and was eventually transferred to another prison for his personal safety.

Still Chad held strongly to his faith. He joined a Bible study class in prison, enrolled in college classes, and led AA meetings.

He called Rhonda two or three times a week and wrote encouraging letters to his family and friends that always ended with the phrase "Faith up" and a hand-drawn picture of a cross engulfed by rays of sunshine. He always reminded his family to be optimistic as they awaited the four-year mark; that was when he would be eligible for early release.

One day Chad telephoned his mom and told her he had injured his knee. The resultant infection had been neglected by the infirmary, and the knee was swollen to the size of an orange.

Four days later, Rhonda received another phone call from Chad. He was upset, crying that something was wrong. The infected knee had grown to the size of a cantaloupe! What's more, he was having difficulty breathing!

Rhonda immediately called the prison, demanding that her son be given medical attention. A coldhearted official told her that if Chad wasn't happy with his health care, he could file a complaint.

Thirty-six hours later Rhonda received a phone call instructing her to come to Arizona as quickly as possible. Chad was in the hospital—on life support!

Accompanied by her youngest son, Jeremy, Rhonda imme-diately flew to Arizona to be with her son. Soon Chad's father and other brothers, Jeff and Brent, gathered at his bedside.

Told that the infection was destroying Chad's vital or-gans, they helplessly watched as Chad fought a valiant fight, but it was beyond his control; he slipped into a coma. Then came the unthinkable: Chad lost his battle to live, a month before Christmas.

It was a nightmare. And simply overwhelming.

❄

The third anniversary of her precious son's graduation to Heaven was approaching like a dark cloud. For the past two years that same dark cloud had hovered over Rhonda like a trip wire ready to extinguish the joy of Christmas. A smiling photo or a fleeting memory of Chad as a happy lit-tle boy on Christmas morning would release pent-up hurt, anger, and tears.

To take her mind off of it, Rhonda started scrolling the Internet. She happened upon the website of items for sale in Minot and began looking at all kinds of Coca-Cola memorabilia.

There were old Coke crates for sale. *How Chad would have loved those*, she thought. An idea suddenly crossed her mind. *Why not buy three of them, one for each of Chad's brothers? It would be such a touching gift, connecting them to their lost sibling.*

Rhonda sent a message to the seller. It turned out that

he had been one of Chad's friends. He said that unfortunately the crates displayed online had already been sold. However, he had other ones that were in better condition and would sell them to her for the same price.

The man subsequently made arrangements for his wife to drop them off at Rhonda's office.

She was excited, knowing she would see them later that day.

When she got to the office, the Coke crates had been delivered and stacked on a chair. As she studied them she noticed that each wooden container had a number. The top carton was number 77.

I'll give that one to Jeff, she thought. *He was born in 1977.*

The next one was 82. *Oh, good. I'll give that to Jeremy, that's his birth year.*

The third one was turned away from her. She felt her heart beating a little faster as she stepped closer to the stack so she could align the last one. She looked. Her eyes widened. It was number 81.

Brent had been born in 1981!

Rhonda sat down, flabbergasted. The divinely aligned numbers took her breath away!

There was no way that seller could have known the birth years of her sons. Yet here she was, gazing at three old Coca-Cola crates with numbers that matched the birth years of each of her surviving boys, who were the recipients of the gifts.

How could it be? What did it mean?

In a flash, Rhonda was given the eyes to see the Godwink.

God had sent her a supernatural message reminding her that Chad was no longer imprisoned but free to walk the streets of Heaven, and that he was now feeling a joy that only God can bring.

> *So if the Son sets you free,*
> *you will be free indeed.*
> —John 8:36 (NIV)

REFLECTIONS

God orchestrated the alignment of those birth dates on the Coke crates in order to provide Rhonda with a special gift of peace and comfort for Christmas that year.

Those divinely aligned numbers on tangible objects associated with Chad were meaningful only to her, her husband, and her surviving sons. God was sending Rhonda a personal message of hope and encouragement, one that only she would get—out of seven billion people on Earth.

God's ability to command the order and alignment of numbers shouldn't be a surprise to us. The cycles of life of every creature on Earth—from the migration of birds to the birth of butterflies—obey God's invisible clocks.

We can see numerical perfection in his every creation: the stars, the sun, and the moon have all been placed at precisely the correct distances for life on Earth to be able to exist.

Lee Strobel once wrote, "The cosmological constant . . . is as precise as throwing a dart from space and hitting a bull's-eye just a trillionth of a trillionth of an inch in diameter on Earth."[1]

Moreover, because God invented time, His omnipotent power can change anything in between the beginning and the end of time.

Think about it.

In your own life, hasn't God used the divine alignment of Godwinks to make Himself known to you—or to reassure you—as He did for Rhonda?

He has set the right time for everything.
He has given us a desire to know the future,
but never gives us the satisfaction of
fully understanding what he does.
—Ecclesiastes 3:11 (GNT)

Molly: Jesus Took the Wheel?

"Don't *should* on yourself," said Molly Nece, smiling as she confidently moved across the stage, delivering one of her favorite lines as a motivational speaker. Her job was to inspire people and equip them with the ability to take charge of their lives and live more intentionally.

She let the words sink in, studying the faces of her audience, watching them go from a momentary jolt to getting her point, then laughing with her.

"How often have you said, 'I *should* have taken that opportunity when it was offered to me'? Don't we go through life saying 'I *should* have done *this* or *should* have done *that*'?"

❊

Days later, Molly was no longer holding a microphone while imparting advice; this time she was standing in her own kitchen, coaching her husband, Dan, who had long wrestled with the question of whether to leave his sales job, which he disliked immensely. She was urging him to consider a new career path.

"Okay," he relented. Then he paused. "But when should you leave a job that brings in a steady paycheck? Now? Just before Christmas? With no path to the future?"

The moment Dan used the word *should*, he could see it coming. Molly was about to utter her classic motivational one-liner. Both of them smiling, they said it in unison: "Don't *should* on yourself!"

That conversation in the kitchen finally motivated Dan to take action. He left his despised job and, as a bridge, took a job for the holidays at a large retail store.

Three weeks before Christmas, his spirits were visibly higher. He even had time to join a men's group at church which helped people in need.

Molly cautioned him that reinventing himself would be a process and there would be a few things he'd have to get used to. She was right. He had to work weekends for the first time in many years and, unlike in his other sales job, he was now on a time clock. Moreover, he had been told that his new employer had no tolerance for employees' being late.

The Sunday before Christmas, Molly and their twelve-year-old son, Tyler, decided to make the best of it while Dan was working.

"Let's go on an adventure, Mom!" said Tyler, wide-eyed. A boy who loved history and nature, he already had an idea of what he wanted to do. "Can we go to Moores Creek Battlefield?" he asked excitedly.

"Good idea," said Molly. "You'll be our navigator. Put it in your GPS, okay?"

Dan's shift at his seasonal job was 10 a.m. to 10 p.m. that Sunday, so Molly and Tyler said their good-byes in the morning and began their adventure.

It was a beautiful day for the forty-five- to sixty-minute drive through North Carolina countryside, up Blueberry Road from Wilmington to Currie, home of the national park commemorating the Revolutionary War battle of Moores Creek.

After an hour or so, Molly and Tyler exited the park to the next leg of their journey, heading northwest. As Molly turned onto the two-lane highway, she noticed that a police car had pulled out behind her. She kept one eye on her speed and the other on the rearview mirror for several miles. The police car made no effort to pass her. When she spotted a gas station up ahead, she decided to pull in to let it pass.

Whew.

She watched as the police car continued on. She pulled back onto the country road, continuing their journey with a little less anxiety.

Molly and Tyler chatted about this and that. Some twenty minutes later, she heard a *ding*. The "low gas" indicator on her dashboard was flashing. *Oh, no!* she thought, instantly reprimanding herself: She *should* have looked at the gas gauge when she pulled into that gas station back there. She *should* have been less occupied with the police car and more focused on necessities.

"Can you check your GPS to see if there's a gas station up ahead, Tyler?" she asked.

"It's not working," he answered a moment later. "There's no GPS signal in this area, Mom!" he said with a bit more urgency.

"Don't worry. It says we have twenty-seven miles before we run out."

A few minutes later they spotted a gas station. "Oh darn," said Molly, reading the sign. "'Closed on Sundays.' Is your GPS working yet?"

"No, still not working."

She looked at the clock. "Does your phone work? Try calling Dad . . . maybe he hasn't left for work yet."

❋

The call went through, and Dan answered. They explained their predicament and asked if he could go on the computer and see if there was a gas station on their route.

He identified one. "No, that's the one we passed a couple miles ago. Closed on Sundays," said Molly.

Then, starting to feel the pressure that he couldn't be late, he said, "I'm sorry, honey, I've got to go. Here's the name and number of another station. If it's too far from you, maybe they can direct you to a station that's closer."

Feeling bad and worried about leaving his wife and son without a solution, he repeated, "I'm really sorry, honey, I've got to go. Would you please leave me a message letting me know how you make out?"

Molly looked at the gas gauge; it was now only ten miles before they would run out. All they could see around them were pine trees.

They pulled over to the side of the road, and Molly's hand was shaking as she dialed the number Dan had given them. A lady with a pleasant voice answered. Molly quickly explained that they were almost on empty and identified their approximate location.

"Don't try to come to us," said the lady confidently. "Just stay on the road you're on. There's a gas station in Wam Squam Bay near White Lake. Try that!"

Tyler watched his mom write down what the lady was saying. When she hung up, he asked, "Mom, why are your hands shaking?"

Molly drew in a breath, then sighed. "Because we're in the middle of nowhere. No other cars are on this road. And all we've seen are trees and a closed gas station!"

Instantly realizing that she was not being strong for her child, she changed the subject. "You know what? Remember that poster we saw the other day? The one that said J-O-Y? Jesus . . . Others . . . and Yourself? We need some JOY . . . some Jesus."

Before resuming their journey, Molly reached out for Tyler's hand, and they prayed together, mother and son. "We need Your comfort and direction, Jesus."

"And a gas station, please," added Tyler.

Molly flashed a smile at her son as she pulled the car back onto the lonely road. "And let's pray it's less than ten miles away."

She was hunched over the wheel, staring at the gauge as every mile crawled by, when another thought passed through her mind. "Remember that Carrie Underwood song on the radio? 'Jesus, Take the Wheel'?"

Tyler nodded.

Trying to ignore the dashboard indicator, which now read five miles to empty, Molly began to sing the chorus: "Jesus, take the wheel, take it from my hands . . . save me from this road I'm on . . ."

She glanced at Tyler. He joined in with her, singing the last line: "Jesus, take the wheel."[1]

"Look at that sign, Mom!" shouted Tyler. "Wam Squam, one mile away!"

As their car rolled into the small gas station, feeling a relief beyond measure, they looked at each other, as if to say, *I think we know who took the wheel!*

❄

Just days before Christmas, Molly and Dan were driving to a restaurant where they had reservations for dinner. It was getting close to dark when Molly spotted a woman looking stressed, walking along the highway. She was carrying a gas container.

"Dan, we need to go back and help that lady."

Dan hesitated. "You sure?" He looked at the clock. "The next exit isn't for half a mile," he told her. "We'll be late."

"Yes! I feel we need to go back. One week ago that could have been Tyler and me."

Dan opened his heart. Without complaint, he took the next exit and headed back.

❄

The woman looked surprised as they pulled up and invited her to get in the car.

"Oh, my, I was just prayin' and prayin' that God would send someone to help me."

Later, as Dan lifted the container to pour the gas into the woman's car, Molly sat inside with her, praying that all stress would be lifted from her shoulders and that she would feel peace during the Christmas holidays.

❄

Outside the car, Dan was feeling an inner joy himself. He thought about that poster that Molly and Tyler had described during their time of stress on the country road. He clearly recalled what they'd told him: it said, JOY equals Jesus, *Others*, and Yourself.

He smiled, glad that Molly had insisted they stop to help that nice woman and realizing that helping other people was boosting his spirits in a very special way.

The kind man who answered the phone at the restaurant assured them their reservation would be honored.

Over dinner, Molly and Dan chatted about what was going on in their lives. Dan revealed that the church men's group had begun to open his eyes to something he'd never really thought too much about. "I've been thinking about your challenge to reinvent myself," he said with a loving look toward his wife. "The men's group has reminded me that my greatest satisfaction comes from helping others. And you shined the light on that again tonight with your instinct that we should go back and help that lady. I'm so glad we did."

Molly smiled demurely, with an infinitesimal shrug. "I guess . . . Jesus took the wheel."

❊

No longer "*should*ing on himself," Dan vowed to start the new year focused on reinventing himself. Over the holidays he had zeroed in on what he'd really like to do. And now he stepped out in faith and began studying for his entrance exam to get into nursing school.

"Our lesson from Christmas that season," reflected Molly, "was that there is always someone worse off than you—someone you can help."

Tyler's takeaway was more basic. He said, "The next time we go on an adventure, we should *print out* directions, too!"

REFLECTIONS

As Molly was becoming more and more anxious, envisioning herself and Tyler stuck in the middle of nowhere with an empty gas tank, she made a choice: instead of letting fear and worry overtake her, she let Jesus take the wheel.

Molly and Tyler decided to fill up their "prayer tank" with petitions to the Lord and hand everything over to Him. What a sense of relief and gratitude when God divinely directed them to a gas station in the nick of time!

The ordeal was fresh in Molly's mind when she saw another woman in the same stressed-out situation. She was empathetic.

The gift of empathy is one of the beautiful characteristics of Jesus. Its origin is found in the Golden Rule, "Do unto others as you would have them do to you." It *always* feels right when you reach out to help others in need.

God used the situation to touch the hearts of Molly, Tyler, Dan, and the lady on the road, letting each one know that when you call out to Him in prayer—He answers.

Have you ever been in a situation when you were gripped with fear? Instead of wasting time fretting and wringing your hands, perhaps you "should have" just prayed.

20

Cathy: Christmas Cookies with Heavenly Delivery

"Christmas cookie time" describes a pair of special days every December at Cathy and Harold Ellis's home, a modest raised ranch house nestled in the northern suburbs of New York City.

For thirty years, Cathy has carried on the tradition inspired by her dear mother. Her memories of being at her mother's side as she turned out the annual batch of holiday sweets were etched in Cathy's memory like a Norman Rockwell painting. Now Cathy had taken on the ambitious job of baking about two thousand cookies every year, resulting in scores of silver trays brimming with colorful crunchy cookies—square cookies, round cookies, and balls—ready to tantalize the taste buds of their eager benefactors, family, and friends.

For her dawn-to-dusk task, Cathy arose early, showered, dressed, and slipped into one of her favorite Christmas aprons. Looking into the mirror over the bureau, she ran a brush through her hair.

Ready, Mom? she asked mentally, glancing at her sweet mother's memorial card tucked into the edge of the mirror. How she missed her mother. The card, inscribed with her mom's name, Lois Jean Morgan, and a few tender words of inspiration, had been given to people attending her funeral three years earlier. *You'll be here with me, Mom*, Cathy resolved, patting the bib over her heart. *Right here*, she repeated inside her mind, *all day today and tomorrow*.

With one more swipe of the brush, Cathy looked at the other memorial cards squeezed into the edge of the mirror. Next to her mom's was that of Harold's mother, Ruth Ellis. She'd been gone seven years now.

Flipping the kitchen lights on, she saw that everything was just as she had prepared it the night before. Her bowls, mixer, flour, and rolling pin were all ready for action. To the side were the metal holders where she would place each tray of fresh-baked cookies as they came out of the oven.

She had a system. Even though it would be more productive to bake multiple trays of cookies simultaneously, she believed each one had its own requirements, so she resolutely baked just one tray at a time.

In her notebook, she would dutifully write down the contents of each tray, noting when a new cookie had entered the annual production line, such as last year's honey sand balls.

Another part of the Ellis Christmas cookie time tradition was to fill the air with holiday music. In the extra bedroom off the kitchen there was a glass cabinet; inside was a CD box with a pull-out drawer. Cathy would revisit that drawer endlessly over the next two days. Her CD player wasn't fancy; it played just one disc at a time.

Harold gave Cathy a wave as he left for work. He knew better than to detain the baker with idle chitchat or, heaven forbid, to enter into the magical cookie factory, which was already producing the olfactory delights of the season.

"Bye! Smells great!" he shouted, heading for the door.

Missing her mom wasn't the only hard part about Christmas cookie time this year. Her daughter, Lori Ann, had landed a job that had moved her to Houston. For years, Lori Ann had been at her side, helping out during this annual event, replicating Cathy's own childhood experiences.

Now Cathy was alone. And feeling it. To heighten her spirits, she went to the CD player and turned up the music, just a little bit louder.

Harold was right. The kitchen smelled wonderful. More than that, it was a festival of sensory delights. She took a moment to appreciate every sense, inhaling the aromas of fresh-baked cookies as she let her eyes pan across the stacks of joyful, colorful treats; her fingers fluttered over the ridges of a crispy cookie before she allowed herself a tasty nibble, while choruses of traditional Christmas harmonies tickled her ears and touched her heart.

I may be physically *alone*, she thought, *but God is allowing me to feel the presence of Mom, right here next to me!*

By midafternoon, Cathy had played her sixth or seventh CD. While transferring the cookies that had cooled into the large Tupperware containers on the dining room table, she realized she was about to hear her dad's favorite holiday song, a parody of "The Twelve Days of Christmas": "The Twelve Pains of Christmas."

She missed her dad too. He'd been gone only fifteen months.

Now Cathy was smiling, anticipating the line that had always tickled her dad. The male singer was poking fun at the complications of putting up the Christmas lights: "One light goes out, they all go out!" He finished big with "Get a flashlight, I blew a fuse!"[1]

Dad would laugh and say, "That's just like me!"

That made her think about her mom again and how much she missed her. *Is it time?* she wondered. *Can I make it through Mom's favorite Christmas song without crying my eyes out?*

Wiping her hands on her apron, Cathy walked into the extra bedroom, opened the glass cabinet, and reached for her mom's favorite CD, "O Holy Night."

She pulled it up, and—what was that? Something else fell out. She lifted it up.

It was another memorial card honoring her mother.

Wha–? How did this get here? I never had two *memorial cards,* she thought, very clearly remembering the one she'd gazed at that morning, stuck into the edge of the mirror on the bedroom bureau. She knew for a fact that it had been there for three years.

Holding the card with a puzzled expression, Cathy shook off her musings, remembering that she had cookies in the oven. She put the CD into the player and walked back to the kitchen.

As she placed more cooled cookies into the containers, her eyes filled with tears, picturing her mom at Christmas, enjoying her favorite song.

Wiping her cheeks with a flour-covered hand, she solemnly listened to the chorus of "O Holy Night," feeling ever so close to her mother, and couldn't help but wonder, *What are the odds of that? Was it some kind of coincidence that another memorial card would appear just like that—or was it something more? Something bigger.*

⁂

When Harold came home from work, she couldn't wait to tell him every detail of what had happened.

"Do you ever remember our having two memorial cards for Mom?" she asked him.

He shook his head.

"It just mysteriously fell into my hand as I was going to play her favorite song," she continued.

At that moment she realized that *her* favorite song was playing, Vince Gill's "Let There Be Peace on Earth." She could never get through that one without choking up and crying.

Her eyes began to fill.

Harold said softly, "I'm sorry you're sad."

"I just really miss my mom. And I especially miss Lori

Ann not being here, listening to Christmas music and baking with me."

Her cell phone rang. It was a video call.

"Hi, Mom," said Lori Ann cheerfully into the screen. "How are you doing without me?"

Cathy thought she was going to stammer and bawl at the same time. In a flash, wonder, disbelief, and astonishment sped through her mind. She had to spill it all out to Lori Ann!

As Harold listened patiently, Cathy repeated the series of Godwink events: that she had been missing her mom, had gone for the CD, and a memorial card of her mom that she'd never known she had had ended up in her hand.

"That's amazing, Mom. Mom? Are you crying?"

"Lori Ann, I'm crying because the song that started playing just as you called is my favorite. And I really miss you and Grams."

Harold took the moment to tell Cathy he was going to get some Christmas CDs for the car.

A few moments later he returned as Cathy and Lori Ann were still having their video chat. He had an astonished look on his face. "Cathy! This is amazing," he said, walking into the kitchen holding several CDs in one hand and something else in the other. "Look what just popped into my hand in the CD cabinet."

Cathy's eyes widened, and her jaw dropped. "Oh, my goodness."

Harold was holding an extra copy of *his* mother's memorial card! She, too, had been an avid baker at Christmastime.

"That's not coincidence," enthused Cathy. "That's God talking to us! Another Godwink!"

And how appropriate: God had divinely aligned the timing of Harold getting home from work and witnessing his own Godwink, in sync with their daughter being on the videophone from 1,700 miles away. Together, the Ellis family experienced God's personal Christmas greeting from above.

❈

As Christmas came and went that year, all the silver trays loaded with crunchy and colorful cookies were delivered on time and were a welcome sight to all family members and friends. Yet few were aware that while Cathy had been baking some two thousand cookies, a wonderful batch of Godwinks had also been baked up in the heavens and sent, special delivery, to Earth for the Ellis Christmas cookie time.

REFLECTIONS

When we lose a loved one, we miss his or her presence here on Earth.

How often have you said, "If only I could hear his voice one more time."

Haven't you longed for one more hug from someone you missed?

God draws you closer to Him when you grieve. He gives

you the hope of Heaven, letting you know that this life is not all there is; we are just "passing through."

To let you know that He feels the pain of your loss and to assure you that one day you'll again see your loved one, he sends sweet signs of connection, such as a gift in a drawer—Godwinks.

> *The LORD is near to the brokenhearted*
> *and saves the crushed in spirit.*
> —PSALMS 34:18 (ESV)

21

Clair: A Picture-Perfect Christmas

One more American hamburger before shipping out for the cold uncertainties of war seemed like a good idea to Clair Miller, a twenty-nine-year-old air force gunner. It was Christmas Eve.

"Let's go," he said to his seven crewmates, salivating at the thought that this might be the last hamburger he'd have for months. He and his buddies were departing California that night for England. From there they'd fly dangerous bombing missions over war-torn Europe.

As one of the oldest crew members, Clair had an almost paternal relationship with the others. His level-headed instinct for leadership—always counseling the younger airmen—had prompted someone to nickname him "Dad." That had stuck.

"All right, fellas, who's hungry?" asked the cute, bouncy waitress. From the pocket of her red-and-white-checkered apron she pulled out a pad, simultaneously extracting a pencil buried in the ringlets of her curly blond hair.

"Anybody going for the Classic Fat Burger?" she asked with a devilish smile. "It's smothered in fried onions, tomato, pickles, and lettuce, with crispy fries on the side."

There was a sudden cacophony of wisecracks and enthusiastic confirmation of orders. One airman was infatuated with the server more than the burger. "What's your name?" he asked, smiling.

"My fiancé, who is already over there fighting this war, calls me 'Sassy Sally.' But you"—she pointed to the grinning airman—"can just call me Sally."

For the next hour, Clair watched as the rambunctious crew dived into their burgers, kidded with Sally, and never let on that they might be the least bit nervous about the mission they were about to undertake.

As the bill came, the eight airmen tossed money onto the table to pay for their share, several telling Sally that it had been a great meal.

"Tell ya what, someone can do me a favor," she said brightly. "Who wants to take a picture of me to my soldier man? He's over there somewhere."

The comment caught them by surprise. Most of them just stared at her, perhaps wondering, *Does she have any idea how many soldiers are "over there" in Europe?*

The crew all looked at "Dad"—Clair.

"Sure, let me have it, Sally," said Clair, not wishing to

disappoint her. He wasn't about to deflate her enthusiasm by lecturing her on the improbability of her request. After all, it was Christmas Eve.

Sally pulled a wallet-sized snapshot from her pocket and handed it to Clair. "Thanks." She smiled. Then, starting to feel the significance of the moment, her face began to squinch as tears formed in the corners of her eyes. She quickly turned, rushing off.

❄

A Classic Fat Burger was a distant memory nine months later when Clair and his crew were in the thick of things. Their missions had come so fast and furious that they could hardly keep track of how many they'd been on. Their B-17 bomber had been attacked by enemy planes and anti-aircraft fire so many times that all they could do was count their blessings that they hadn't been seriously hit.

Then one day, over the Netherlands, things changed.

The plane was rocked by a powerful explosion, and soon the aircraft spun out of control as the pilot ordered everyone to bail out! As Clair's chute snapped open, he heard another explosion. Their B-17 had blown up!

As soon as Clair's feet touched the ground, he rolled and quickly released the parachute harness. He stood and looked around; none of his crewmates was anywhere in sight.

As he searched for the best way to escape, he suddenly found himself staring at the barrels of six enemy rifles.

German soldiers rushed toward him, roughly pushing him toward their encampment, where they tied him to a tree. He spent the cold night without food, water, or covering.

Before dawn, Clair was dragged into the center of a dirt road and ordered to stand. The leader commanded the six soldiers to aim their rifles at him. A second command in German was shouted . . . to get ready.

Clair knew that the final command would be the end. He looked his captors in the eye. He had but one choice: to ask God for assistance. Inside his mind, he said, "Please, God, save me."

Abruptly he heard the voices of teenage girls. The trio ran toward the firing squad, shouting in Dutch, "Don't shoot! He's a Yank, not a Brit!"

Remarkably, those girls had come from nowhere. How had they gotten the courage to shout at a German firing squad?

No one knows—nor why Clair's nationality would have made a difference—but the soldiers lowered their guns, and Clair's prayer was answered. Temporarily he was saved.

But soon he was shoved into a crowded train boxcar and transported to a prisoner-of-war camp called Stalag Luft 4, somewhere behind German lines.

❄

The days passed slowly. Food was not plentiful. The POW barracks, stretching as far as the eye could see, were cold, damp, and drafty. Blankets were hard to come by.

As winter approached, the temperatures slid into the twenties. Many young men became ill or fell into a deep depression. Some elected to run into the electric fences, causing themselves instant death by electrocution, rather than endure the continued harshness of their fate.

As was his paternalistic nature, Clair worried less about himself than about those around him. Once again, his innate leadership qualities caused others to turn to him for counsel and encouragement. They trusted this "more mature" American airman, who seemed secure in his faith and values.

As Clair counseled one soldier after another, he sought to leave everyone with hope. He shared stories of those who had overcome difficult circumstances in order to help build the faith of his listeners.

As Christmas approached, he knew his fellow prisoners could easily spiral into deeper depression. But his intention was to use the coming holiday as a symbol of hope. He reasoned that if he could get them thinking about the wonderful holiday gatherings at home, he would give them a motivation to persist against adversity and to believe that God would indeed manage their freedom—perhaps getting them back home in time for the next Christmas.

"There's a young man you should see," whispered one POW to Clair urgently. "He's an American—talking about suicide."

As Clair walked to see the young man, he realized that it was one year to the day that he and his crew members had enjoyed that last meal on American soil. It was once again Christmas Eve.

The nineteen-year-old was downcast and huddled on his bunk. "I'm going to ram into that electric fence," he muttered with an angry voice.

"Why would you want to do that?" asked Clair quietly.

"What's the use?" asked the dejected young man. "We're going to die here anyway—why not get it over with?"

Clair sat down on the bed beside him. "You don't want to do that," he said. "This is Christmas Eve. This is the night that hope was born, not a time for hope to be lost."

The young man was quiet.

"Do you like music?" asked Clair, trying to get the other man's thoughts onto something else.

The young man remained quiet.

Clair didn't rush him. He just waited.

"Yeah, I used to play saxophone," murmured the young man.

"Really? I love the sound of a saxophone," said Clair quietly, beginning to move the young man's attention away from his woes. "You like baseball?" he asked.

"Yeah."

"What team?"

"The Cubs."

That was a new pathway of distraction. Clair talked about a time he had gone to a game. His favorite team, the Cincinnati Reds, had lost to the Chicago Cubs.

After a while, a conversation was simply taking place between two American servicemen far away from home.

"My name is Clair Miller," he said, stretching out a hand.

"I'm Ronnie. Ronnie Simpson."

There was a momentary pause. Then Ronnie looked at Clair and asked a question of his own. "You married?"

"Yes, I am," said Clair. "Would you like to see a picture of my wife?"

Ronnie nodded and watched as Clair pulled a picture of his wife from his wallet and showed it to him. But the young man's eyes averted. He became distracted as something else fell to the floor. He leaned to pick it up. It was another picture. He was shocked! "Where did you get this?" he demanded.

Ronnie's change of attitude startled Clair. Then the memory came back to him: Ronnie was holding the picture of Sally, the waitress, that he'd tucked into his wallet exactly one year ago.

"That's the girl I'm going to marry. How did you get this?" repeated the young man sternly.

Clair was suddenly the one who was speechless. Finally he drew in a breath and said, "Ronnie, a few minutes ago we were talking about hope. Hope comes from God. And the evidence of faith and hope is the amazing things that only He can do, that are beyond human comprehension. You and I, at this very moment, are witnessing one of His miracles."

Clair went on to explain to Ronnie that last Christmas Eve, in a little diner in California, a sweet waitress named Sally had told of her boyfriend who was fighting for his country. She had demonstrated enormous faith by asking a bunch of strangers, who were going off to war, to deliver a picture of herself to her fiancé.

"She didn't even tell us your name, Ronnie. Think of that—Sally had such faith in God that she knew He would lead me to you, to give you something of hope—a picture of her." He put a hand on Ronnie's shoulder. "God knows right where you are, Ronnie. Think of that!"

Clair stood and took a mental snapshot that he would carry in his heart forever: the scene of Ronnie sitting on the edge of his bed, gazing at the photo of his girlfriend, Sally. And on his face was the look of hope.

"Merry Christmas, Ronnie," said Clair, walking away. *Thank you, God*, he said on the inside.

❄

The rest of the story?

Both Clair and Ronnie returned home safely. They got there in time for the next Christmas. Ronnie and Sally were married. And, according to letters received from them by Clair, they lived happily ever after.

REFLECTIONS

This young soldier had lost his will to live and desperately needed a handrail of hope. What were the odds that a photo of his fiancée would travel thousands of miles and "accidentally" fall out of Clair's pocket?

There are no odds, accidents, happenstance, or coincidences with God. That strategically placed photo became a lifeline for a despondent man.

You may have called *your* Godwinks "coincidences" at one time, but now you know they are sweet messages, directly to you, from a loving God.

We've learned that when you share your Godwink stories with others, it encourages them to share *their* Godwink stories. As you gather around the holiday table, let your conversation honor God by giving testimony to what He has done. Godwinks are the gifts that keep on giving!

> *Go home to your friends and tell them*
> *how much the Lord has done for you.*
>
> —MARK 5:19 (ESV)

22

Greg: A Loving Piece
of Christmas Pie

For more than thirty years, Greg Glauser has been a dedicated teacher at the Brookwood Community west of Houston, where 125 adults with disabilities joyfully live and work.

He organizes all the social activities for the citizens, leads the Sunday chapel services, and—his biggest job of the year—organizes the annual Christmas Open House performances.

That weekend, thousands of visitors flock to Brookwood to buy their Christmas poinsettias and gift items, have lunch at the café, and attend one of the citizen performances.

Of course, as mentioned earlier in this book, most people agree that whenever you visit Brookwood Community during the year, you feel something akin to the Christmas spirit.

Once Christmas Open House weekend is over, Greg rests a little and just focuses on enjoying the Christmas holiday.

A widower, he eats most of his meals at fast-food restaurants and therefore welcomes being invited to homemade meals with family and friends at Christmastime. "I particularly love it when they serve green bean casserole and baked macaroni and cheese," he says.

But the highlight is dessert.

Greg explains, "My dear wife, Andrea, who passed away many years ago, used to bake one cherry pie and one apple pie, every Thanksgiving and Christmas." With a melancholy look on his countenance, he continues, "I fondly remember our dessert time. We would always have a slice of both and go over the many blessings of our lives."

❋

One holiday weekend Greg was invited to two dinners. He was excited. He was given the green bean casserole at one person's house and the macaroni and cheese at the other.

Yet, for dessert, he felt a twinge of disappointment. "They served wonderful homemade apple pie—but no cherry pie."

When he returned home that evening, he scolded himself. *Perhaps it's just a silly tradition, having both apple and cherry pie in remembrance of the wonderful times I had with Andrea.*

The next day, Greg told one of his colleagues, Mary, about his experience. Trying to laugh it off, he said, "Perhaps cherry pies simply aren't 'in' this year."

That day Mary was working at one of the homes for citizens. She perked up when someone said that a nice bakery in town had sent some pies to share with the Brookwood Community. She watched carefully as the cart was unloaded. She saw all kinds of pies. But no cherry pie.

Then, at the last moment, there it was! *One cherry pie!*

"Please, can we give that to Greg?" she asked.

Greg was so excited when Mary knocked on the door and handed him the cherry pie. "I took it to my kitchen, sat down, and cut into it immediately," he later said with a smile.

But he knew that that cherry pie was very special; it had been delivered as a Christmas Godwink. "With each bite I counted my blessings, looked up, and said 'Hello' to my wonderful wife in Heaven." He then added, "I savored every thought of her. And every bite!"

REFLECTIONS

God has given us the ability to recall the little things in life that bring us joy. When Greg remembered the good times he had had with his beloved wife, he was also remembering how much God loves him.

Memories are gifts—treasures that we keep in our hearts. They will never collect dust or rust or be stolen. They will be with us forever—even into eternity.

Many . . . are the wonders you have done,
the things you planned for us.

—Psalms 40:5 (NIV)

23

Ted: Turning Christmas Blues into Joy

It was an hour before dawn and still dark.

Unable to sleep, Ted strained to sit up in bed, struggling with the familiar heaviness of the unbearable, inescapable, unrelenting sadness that had weighed him down for one year to the day.

Prior to this day a year ago, Ted could at least cling to a thin thread of hope. Then—the thread had snapped.

How he had hated to have to make that decision, to have to put his "precious angel," Kathy, into hospice care on the eve of her favorite holiday, Christmas.

Am I calling for assistance too early? he had wondered, questioning the apparent insensitivity of the timing. *Will the children forever remember their mother's special holiday as the time that Dad called in hospice?*

But what choice did he have? The ravages of ovarian cancer had claimed Kathy's body. Every doctor and every adviser had said there were no more options, there was no hope. And though she was close to dying, no one could have known that she was so close to the end.

Still, did I do all that I could?

Then, in the morning darkness, Ted remembered his dear friend Jack Kiser, with whom he had talked on the phone the day before. Jack, who had also lost his wife to cancer, had seriously advised Ted, "Don't do what I did. I waited too long to put my wife into hospice."

That's when Ted knew he needed help. *God, don't let me get in Your way*, he had prayed silently.

The hospice had been wonderful. The skilled professionals there had responded quickly with a hospital bed and pharmaceutical supplies. They hadn't immediately assigned a hospice attendant, but they had patiently guided Ted through this uncharted experience, providing him with careful instructions on how to medicate Kathy as needed.

Ted shuddered as he replayed the prior Christmas Eve in his mind.

Kathy had begun to cry out. The new medication was making her delirious, and she kept trying to get out of bed. Finally, after what seemed like hours, her eyes closed. But then Ted began to worry that perhaps she had gone into a coma. He was tormented, wondering if she would wake up.

What if I didn't get to say good-bye? he thought, and a lump formed in his throat so big that it hurt.

Distraught, he leaned his head on his hands. Soon he succumbed to exhaustion and slept on the floor for a few hours.

When he awoke on Christmas morning, Kathy was sitting up in bed!

"Morning, honey!"

She was alert! More alert than she had been in weeks!

"Do you have those books I bought for the boys?" she asked, referring to their grandchildren.

"Yes, of course," said Ted, puzzled by her odd but welcome turnaround. He got the books right away. They were identical copies of *The Night Before Christmas*. By clicking a button, she could read the story aloud and record it so the child could play it back over and over again. In a clear voice Kathy read both books all the way through. Ted was astonished by her stamina.

As he wrapped the books in bright red paper, he couldn't help but think, given the circumstances, what a treasure the books would be for those boys. Long into the future, they would be able to hear the classic Christmas tale told in their grandmother's gentle voice.

Later that day, Christmas afternoon, Kathy weakened. That time, she slipped into a coma from which she never returned.

❄

The first anniversary of the loss of a loved one is always a mighty test of faith. As much as you'd like to avoid it, that date creeps toward you like an ominous dark cloud before a storm. You hope it'll just pass you by—quickly.

Ted put on his robe and walked into the den, illuminated only by the lights on the tree.

Before going to bed, he had finished the decorating, trying to put everything into exactly the place where Kathy would have wanted them. She was known for decorating to the hilt. There was hardly a spot—inside or outside the house—that didn't celebrate the birthday of Jesus.

Ted hung the stockings over the fireplace, draped the garlands here and there, and, very carefully—as she had always reminded him—threaded the special family ornaments onto sturdy branches, making certain they were secure.

Now, in the slight chill of morning, in front of the fire-place, he dropped into a chair and reassessed his decorating accomplishments in the dim, multicolored light from the tree.

As Ted studied the decor, he couldn't help but smile at the memory of Kathy's holiday exuberance. At this time of year, she had been like a grown-up kid.

As if he were pulling snapshots from a mental album, he pictured her Christmas ritual of handing out personalized ornaments to Ted and each of the children. Those ornaments had now multiplied to two or three dozen. Each had a prominent place on the tree, except for the ornament she had given to Ted one season, the little ceramic picture frame that sat on the table beside his chair. Kathy had been afraid that the frame might be a little too heavy to hang on the tree, so she had always set it on the side table next to a Christmas candle.

As Ted gazed at the ornament, his eyes started to moisten. Inside the frame was Kathy's smiling face—just the way everyone remembered her. Kathy always smiled. Her photo was flanked by ceramic red-and-white candy canes, and across the top of the frame were the words *Merry Christmas.*

Oh, how Ted missed her. *God, please help me get through this holiday.*

He knew that if he pushed the little button at the top of the picture frame, it would play a recorded message.

He recalled that you had to press it with a fingernail, just right, to get it to work.

But he didn't dare do that. He couldn't bear to hear Kathy's voice. He had teared up the first time he heard it—and every year since. He knew that if he pushed that button now, he would cry like a baby.

Oh, God . . . if only she were here . . .

Forcing his thoughts in another direction, Ted decided that it was still too dark in the room. Kathy always said that candlelight warmed up a room, so he pulled himself from the chair, went to the fireplace, picked up the lighter, and flicked the flame to light each of the candles on the mantel. Returning to his chair, he flicked the lighter again to ignite the candle on the side table, next to Kathy's picture.

Suddenly he was jolted! It was as if an electric shock had run through him. Kathy's voice was coming from the picture frame!

"Wha—?"

Ted's mind searched for an explanation. *I didn't touch that frame. All I did was light the candle next to it!*

Again he flicked the lighter to ignite the candle, and again the voice of his dear wife came from the picture frame, mysteriously filling the quiet of the room!

Ted fell into the chair. And cried.

A few minutes later, he tried to sort it out. As a high school teacher and coach, he knew there must be a scientific reason for that phenomenon. Yet there was no accounting for the amazing timing—the divine alignment of his receiving this remarkable Godwink connection to his "precious angel" just when he needed it most—and just after he had said to God, in an unintentional prayer, "If only she were here."

A peace that surpassed all understanding began to flow over Ted. He knew that this was a Christmas Godwink he would never forget. He knew that God—and possibly his "angel" from Heaven, Kathy herself—was sending a personal link of joy to lift his spirits.

So, one more time, Ted flicked the lighter, this time giving it full attention as Kathy's sweet voice filled the room: "Merry Christmas, honey. I love you very much. Happy New Year."

Ted smiled. Almost giddy with joy, he flicked the lighter near to the frame again and again.

"Merry Christmas to you too, my darling wife. I'll see you in eternity—and I'll love you forever and ever."

✻

Ted Harris believes that although his prayers that morning were unintentional—he wasn't on his knees with folded hands, intentionally speaking to God—he was nonetheless in a state of prayer that had carried him through many days of grief.

Ted often chatted intentionally and directly with God, and he had definitely felt God's presence during Kathy's last days this side of eternity.

✻

The rest of the story . . .

A year and a half after Kathy graduated to Heaven, Ted was still visibly grieving. Old friends who lived near Fort Worth, Texas, Larry and Linda Jackson, decided to throw a party for him to cheer him up. Ted felt he had no choice but to go, so he drove up from Houston to attend.

As he entered their home, he saw the banner. It said, "Give Ted a Hug Party."

One of the persons who had been invited was Jan Mc-Neill, one of Ted's classmates at Texas Christian University forty years before. Their conversation rekindled fond memories. Jan had been quite content with her single status for twenty-two years, but Ted's warm personality and sense of humor reminded her of the years gone by. They began to date, and six months later they were married and began a new chapter in each of their lives.

REFLECTIONS

God's omnipresence is a gift. Even if you are not speaking directly to God, He loves you so much that He feels your every hurt and knows every tear you shed. He looks at your losses, disappointments, conflicts, and sorrows with compassion and love. So even if you don't intentionally pray to Him, God knows what kind of comfort you need exactly when you need it.

> *You keep track of all my sorrows.*
> *You have collected all my tears in your bottle.*
> *You have recorded each one in your book.*
>
> —PSALMS 56:8 (NLT)

24

Brooke and Luke: Expecting
a Wonderful Life

I n the classic Christmas film *It's a Wonderful Life*,
George Bailey flirts with pretty Mary Hatch as they
walk along the quiet streets in the fictional town of Bedford Falls.

Jimmy Stewart, in the role of George, jocularly brags
that he's going to travel the world. Trying to impress
Donna Reed, who plays Mary, he then says he's going
to build skyscrapers and bridges. No dream is too big.
Then he asks her a question: "What is it you want, Mary?
You—you want the moon? Just say the word and I'll throw
a lasso around it and pull it down. . . . I'll give you the
moon, Mary."

Loving everything about this big-thinking suitor, Mary
replies with a twinkle and a smile, "I'll take it! Then what?"[1]

It's a Wonderful Life has become the most televised and
one of the most popular movies of all time.[2] Yet, despite

the torrent of postwar optimism when it opened in 1947, the film was a box-office flop. What's more, after Liberty Films went belly-up, the movie was written off as a half-million-dollar loss.

Adding insult to injury, a clerical error in the 1970s allowed the film to slip into the public domain, meaning that TV stations everywhere could air it for free for two decades until the copyright was finally restored in the 1990s.

Yet many, in hindsight, believe that clerical error was a Godwink. They reason that it was the constant televising of *It's a Wonderful Life* every holiday, for free, by thousands of TV stations that boosted its visibility and kept it alive in the hearts of millions of fans.

This we know: Jimmy Stewart and director Frank Capra both said it was their all-time favorite movie. Seventy-one years later, both of them would have been pleased; on Christmas Eve 2017, *It's a Wonderful Life*, now under a long exclusive contract with NBC, was the highest-rated show on US television.

❅

Brooke Smith, an attractive, bright twenty-five-year-old millennial who was making her way in the New York media world as a budding network television reporter, had never seen the classic movie.

That was about to change. Let's rewind to four months earlier, August 2017.

Brooke was catching up with a college roommate who trod on sensitive territory; she asked about her personal life.

"Personal life?" asked Brooke, repeating her standard answer to that question: "TV people *have* no life." She laughed animatedly. "No television just for pleasure, no books unless you're doing work research. And dating? Forget about it." Slipping into a more serious tone, she admitted, "I haven't been on a date in a year. I hate dating." She went on to rail about online dating services.

"Have you tried Hinge?" asked her friend. Brooke shook her head. "It's a new dating service for millennials. They narrow the candidates by personality, common interests, and proximity."

Gun-shy and doubtful, Brooke later thought about it, then reluctantly downloaded the app.

Luke's picture came up right away. He was handsome, and his profile said he worked in commercial real estate and was located, as she was, in Midtown. He didn't drink, didn't smoke, and had been raised in a home with faith. Soon Brooke and Luke were texting each other, both confessing that they were wary of dating services.

Luke told Brooke that he'd gotten a new job that very day. His office would soon be located in the Wall Street area, downtown.

After a day or two of text messaging, they decided to meet after work at a Midtown rooftop restaurant. They hit it off right away, jabbering joyfully about a multitude of mutual interests. Luke told Brooke that his favorite Christmas movie was one she'd never seen, *It's a Wonderful Life*. She told him that hers was *Miracle on 34th Street*.

As they talked about Luke's new job downtown, they speculated whether the dating app Hinge would have even matched them up had they waited a day or two later to sign up, now that their jobs were more geographically distant. A thought flickered through each of their minds as to whether it was some kind of Godwink, but, for the time being, the possibility that they had been divinely aligned to be at the right place at the right time was left unmentioned.

As Christmas approached, Brooke and Luke became more and more comfortable with each other, texted daily, and spent more time together. Soon they were talking about meeting each other's families.

One evening, filled with the joy of the season, they walked arm in arm near the Christmas tree in Rockefeller Center, past festively decorated buildings up Fifth Avenue, and along the south side of Central Park lined with horse-drawn carriages. Love and holiday spirit were in the air. Pinching themselves over their good fortune and warm feelings for each other, they felt like a couple in a romantic movie.

Luke's mind whimsically drifted to his favorite line in his favorite movie, when Jimmy Stewart was showing off to Donna Reed as they walked along a decorated street in Bedford Falls, and here *they* were, walking along a fabled Manhattan street. He couldn't stop himself.

YOU ARE NOW IN BEDFORD FALLS

"You want the moon? Just say the word, and I'll throw a lasso around it and pull it down. I'll give you the moon, Brooke," said Luke with enthusiasm.

Brooke melted instantly. *That* was the most romantic thing she had ever heard!

Moments later she melted again. Luke had stopped, looked at her, and said, "I love you, Brooke."

There was an instant fullness in her throat as tears began to form in her eyes. "I love you, too," she heard herself say.

❄

After hearing Luke quote Jimmy Stewart's line from *It's a Wonderful Life*, Brooke felt that she absolutely had to see that movie. Now it was a quest. In the days leading up to Christmas, she and Luke tried several times to find it. But it wasn't available. They would have to wait until NBC's Christmas Eve telecast, and they had already decided that they wouldn't spend that evening together—it was still too soon in their relationship—and would instead be with their own families.

As a consolation, the weekend before Christmas they decided to watch Brooke's favorite Christmas film, *Miracle on 34th Street*. As the movie approached her favorite scene, she excitedly anticipated it: "Oh, watch this! I've loved this scene since I was five."

The mother, played by Maureen O'Hara, was opening her Christmas present. She pulled out a pair of copper-colored gloves. "I *love* those!" exclaimed Brooke.

A few days later, their last chance to be together before departing for the holiday, they exchanged gifts. Brooke was flabbergasted! The package Luke handed her contained a pair of copper-colored gloves! Once more, she melted.

❄

The new year had barely begun as Brooke sat in her apartment assessing how her life had changed in just six months. Love had blossomed after hope had dwindled. Optimism and joy had pushed aside weariness and wondering. Now she was looking into the future with confidence and more certainty.

Still, a question arose in her mind: *Is this too good to be true?*

Immediately swiping away negative thoughts, she grabbed her phone, a habit of distraction. The screen was notifying her of a post from the Timehop app; one of its regular features was appearing, "On This Day in Your History." She felt momentarily confused as she stared at a quote she herself had posted six years ago to that very day.

The words—from years before she had met Luke—were now familiar. They said:

> You want the moon? Just say the word, and I'll throw a lasso around it and pull it down. . . . I'll give you the moon.

It took her breath away!

A feeling of peace came over Brooke as she smiled. She had just been Godwinked—big time!

REFLECTIONS

Frank Capra once told the *New York Times* that despite his creative and artistic impulses, he felt that the worth of a film was determined not by his audiences but "by the approval of the one man at the top."

Perhaps Capra understood the thesis of Godwinks in this book: that God will use any number of methods to get your attention, sometimes even speaking to you through famous lines from the movies!

Godwinks are gifts of reassurance to give you hope and encouragement during times of uncertainty, helping to move you toward certainty. That includes one of life's greatest challenges: finding your perfect love!

Brooke and Luke now feel that reassurance. As they discuss homes, perfect weddings, and places to travel to, Brooke says, "We daydream together of all of the love and happiness that the future holds."

> *It is not good for the man to be alone.*
> *I will make a helper who is just right for him.*
> —GENESIS 2:18 (NLT)

25

Diane: Godwinked by the Darndest Things

It was a windy, dreary early December morning in the St. Paul suburb, a weighty gray day that heaped itself onto Diane and Rob Baum during an already difficult period in their lives.

As she looked out the window, wind gusts were stirring up leaves as something white whipped through the air, catching her attention, then landing, stuck, and waving tauntingly from a small tree. It was an ugly plastic bag.

I don't like trash waving to me from my trees! sputtered Diane inside her head.

Why that annoyed her so much, she wasn't sure. But, since Rob had unfairly lost his truck-driving job, she became annoyed more easily. They had told him they were letting him go because his blood pressure was too high for state regulations. Yet by the time the doctor prescribed medication to manage his blood pressure, his job had already been filled by somebody else.

That annoyed her. It wasn't fair.

Subsequently, every other job he had applied for seemed to have dozens of applicants and had been filled by someone who had gotten there sooner.

She had faith, strong faith. And she had developed the ability to see God's hand in so many things that others would dismiss. For instance, in walking Captain, her dog, the week earlier, she had spotted a penny on the ground and picked it up. That was something she wouldn't have been inclined to do before things got tight. Now she found herself looking upward with gratitude.

"It's only a penny, but thank you, God."

Then, as if God were answering her with a string of Godwinks, she kept on finding coins on the ground. By the time she returned home, she had twenty-three cents!

She told Rob that she was sure God was trying to get their attention. She just knew something good was going to happen, something with hope and encouragement.

And a job attached.

Her enthusiasm suddenly deflated. She remembered that her kids had excitedly phoned to say they were all coming for Christmas. She was glad. She didn't want to rain on their parade. But she quietly wondered where she and Rob would get the money for food, drinks, and presents.

Now here she was, standing in the kitchen, looking through the window as a white plastic bag thumbed its nose at her. *That* was an annoyance she could do something about! She grabbed a jacket and marched out the door, pulling the jacket tightly around her as she strode down the driveway, a woman on a mission.

The wind gusts were strong, but by straining, with a stick in her hand, she victoriously snatched the pesky plastic intruder. She stuffed it into her pocket, saving it for the trash can.

"Hey, Diane!"

She looked toward her neighbor's house. It was Scott, walking toward her.

That surprised her. Because of Scott's work schedule, they saw him only on rare occasions. Now here he was, coming out to be neighborly on a crummy day.

"Is Rob still looking for work?" he asked, bracing against the wind.

Diane nodded. "Unfortunately, yes."

He handed her a piece of paper with a phone number. She took it, holding it tightly to keep it from blowing away.

"I happen to be off today. I was talking with a friend who says he needs a truck driver for six to eight weeks. His regular driver is out with health issues. It's only temporary, but do you think Rob would be interested?"

Her mind swam with excitement. "Yes!" she declared. "That's great. Thank you, Scott!" she shouted, grinning and already moving toward the house. "I'll have Rob call right away. Thank you so much!"

"Only temporary" will fill the gap through Christmas and bridge us into the new year, thought Diane as she walked briskly toward the house.

Bustling into the kitchen, she tossed the plastic bag into the trash container as she told Rob what had happened. Within minutes he was on the phone, calling the number. They hired him right away, and the following day he started his temporary job.

"It was enough to give us a wonderful Christmas with the kids that year," said Diane later. "As I looked at the gifts under the tree and Christmas dinner on the table, I gave thanks to God for His wonderful bounty."

❄

Rob's temporary employment stretched into February. And by that time, Diane was certain that God was cooking up something else—a real surprise.

One morning she was chatting with God as usual, in prayer, while walking Captain. She had an overwhelming feeling in her spirit that she had absolutely nothing to worry about. As she arrived back at the house, Rob was smiling. He'd just gotten a call from his brother, who still lived in their hometown, three hours away in Minnesota. "He told me there was a custodial job available at my old high school. What do you think?"

"I'm thinking that maybe our prayers are going to be answered," Diane replied brightly.

Rob went online to apply for the job, got a positive response, and soon drove back to Minnesota for his job interview. He thought it had gone well. But until the school completed its process, there was nothing he could do but wait.

Four or five weeks crept by. Easter was around the corner.

Rob was starting to get discouraged. "They didn't call me back right away, so maybe I didn't get it," he reasoned dourly.

Diane struggled to bolster his faith while holding on to her own. Every day, she walked the dog. Every day, she spoke with God, asking for a sign. Walking toward home one morning, she repeated her plea. "I really need a sign, God—just a little sign, please?"

She passed a big trash bin. Sitting on top was a large, clean box that hadn't been there when she'd started her walk. She felt an inner compulsion to grab it.

"Hmmm. Are you trying to tell me something, God? Maybe *that box* is our sign," she said to Captain. She grabbed it and lugged it home.

Rob was standing at the kitchen counter. "What's that for?"

"For packing. I'm getting ready to *move*."

"Really?"

R-i-n-g. It was Rob's phone. The caller ID said the call was from Minnesota.

Diane wore a tight-lipped smile as she slowly carried the box toward the bedroom while listening to Rob on the phone. She could hear a brightness in his voice.

"The Monday after Easter? Sure, I could start then."

Now she grinned. That box was her sign. "Thank you, God."

Rob told her the job was his! They both got packing!

You are really amazing, God, thought Diane. *You had everything lined up perfectly. And You used trash, of all things, to give me Godwink signs!*

REFLECTIONS

God let Diane know that He had her back by using an unexpected object—a worthless plastic bag. He caused the wind to whip the bag through the air, both to command her attention and to land on just the right branch of a tree, where she could reach it. That enabled the neighbor to spot her and be motivated to deliver good news about a job opportunity for Rob.

Later, God repeated Himself, again using something perceived as worthless—a cardboard box tossed into a trash bin—to get Diane's attention.

❄

When we stay tuned in to God, He tunes in to us and lifts our worries. And even the most insignificant and worthless things can become His tools to let you know that He's looking out for you.

We need to stay alert and develop the eyes to see every Godwink that unfolds in our lives. Sometimes they're great, sometimes they're small—such as a worthless plastic bag—but each one is important, because they can lead to a gift from Him.

> *Do not worry about your life,*
> *what you will eat or drink . . .*
> *look at the birds of the air . . .*
> *your heavenly Father feeds them.*
> *Are you not much more valuable than they?*
> —MATTHEW 6:25–26 (NIV)

26

Cindy and Katelynn: An Unforgettable Christmas Wink

It was after 8 a.m. on a mid-September morning, just a few days into the new school year.

Substitute teacher Cindy Santos slid behind the wheel of her car and began the ten-minute drive from her home in Blandon in central Pennsylvania to Richmond Elementary School.

Cindy liked subbing. The scheduling flexibility fit the needs of her busy household with her husband, Matt, and her three boys, aged thirteen to eighteen. She also enjoyed the variety of going from class to class, from school to school.

Driving familiar back roads flanked by picturesque farmlands, she considered that today—her first assignment of the year—would be both a treat and a challenge. Overseeing a class of cute kindergartners ought to be fun.

Then she had second thoughts: it was an unusually large class—twenty-seven kids. *This may be pretty tough*, she thought with a sigh. *Many of those children, unaccustomed to school, will still be missing their moms and dads.*

Cindy said a prayer: *I'm relying on You for guidance today, God!*

As it turned out, it would be the *only* time in the entire school year that Cindy would oversee a kindergarten class. Yet it would be her most amazingly auspicious school day ever!

❋

Elsewhere in central Pennsylvania, Chris and Alicia Ernst's household was bustling with morning activity. Their older daughter, eleven-year-old Kayla, caught her bus to middle school around eight o'clock. With the help of eight-year-old Kameryn, Alicia was readying five-year-old Katelynn for the 8:45 bus to Richmond Elementary. Ever since Katelynn had gotten sick, Kameryn had relished the role of big sister. Every day she watched out for Katelynn all the way to school and all the way home.

Alicia, who had given birth to her fourth child a year earlier—a little boy, Noah—had a definite routine as she dressed Katelynn. She carefully folded the twelve-inch tube into a horseshoe shape, bandaged it to Katelynn's tummy, secured the open end of the tube with tape, and hid it under her child's top. It was through that tube that Katelynn received dialysis for her kidney failure ten hours every night from 8 p.m. to 6 a.m.

The only interruption would be if the machine acted up during the night and Alicia had to get up, clean it, and reactivate it. Such an occurrence would extend Katelynn's treatment into the morning, for she needed to complete the required ten hours of dialysis each day.

❄

Alicia's husband, Chris, allowed himself a half hour for his drive to work, arriving at the bank by 9 a.m.

The daily commute was a sanctuary for him, one of the few times during the day when he was totally alone. At home, he was dad, husband, breadwinner, and Mr. Steady Hand.

"He is my rock," Alicia is fond of saying. "I'm a wreck, but he's the strong one."

But during the solitude of the morning drive, Chris didn't have to wear his typical attitude of optimism. He had thirty minutes to sort through matters of concern—the mounting medical bills, his constant worry that his darling little girl had a death sentence hanging over her, and his frustration that Alicia and he were still desperately trying to find Katelynn a kidney donor.

Alone in the car, Chris could cry out to God, even rail at Him, when he saw other children who had started treatment at the same time Katelynn did but were already being healed of kidney failure. Or when he learned that people who had answered his Facebook plea for a kidney donor for his daughter later confided that they had contacted the hospital and never heard back.

"Shouldn't they have more people answering the phone?" he asked Alicia.

Lately his faith was beginning to fade. From behind the steering wheel, he shouted, "Where *are* You in all this, God?"

❋

Before walking into the classroom at Richmond School, Cindy Santos had a short chat with the school nurse, Doreen, a friend, who told her that one little girl in her class would need special attention.

There she was, petite, auburn-haired Katelynn Ernst with alluring and sleepy brown eyes.

She's so cute! Who could not love that child? thought Cindy, feeling an instant compassion for the little girl.

According to the nurse, Katelynn had been awaiting a kidney transplant for many months, was on dialysis ten hours a day, and took twelve daily medications.

Cindy found herself drawn to the little girl who was quieter than the others.

❋

The day with the kindergartners came and went. The next morning, Cindy was off to another classroom at another school. Another twenty or twenty-five young faces that she couldn't possibly remember or even get to know. Yet, despite her hectic life of a substitute teacher, there was something peaceful about the occasional moments when the image of sweet little Katelynn floated through her mind.

Ten days later, a Godwink happened.

Cindy was scrolling through the Facebook page of a friend when an image labeled "Katelynn's Kidney Journey" popped up in the right-hand column.

(Was that a divinely aligned Godwink?)

I wonder if this is the same Katelynn, thought Cindy, clicking the icon.

There she was! The same little girl with those remarkably engaging brown eyes and, in this picture, a slight smile. Cindy read with interest the heartfelt notes of well-wishers, all hoping that Katelynn would soon find a kidney donor. Her parents had written about the difficulty of locating a perfect match. Everyone in Katelynn's family and many family friends had been scratched off the list of possible donors.

Cindy read the initial requirements: compatible blood type, A or O; good health; age between eighteen and seventy.

Hmm . . . I could be a fit, thought Cindy.

She saw a telephone number to call for more information. She stared at it a moment—and then promptly logged off Facebook.

❋

The following evening, Cindy was still thinking about Katelynn. She decided to tell her husband, Matt, about having met her. They talked about how hard it must be for the parents of a sick child to let go and send their daughter to school; how concerned they must be for her.

Cindy admitted to Matt that the little girl had remained on her mind. "How would you feel about me calling that number and exploring the matter further?" she asked gently.

Understanding his wife's curiosity, Matt looked at her compassionately and said, "It can't hurt to get more information."

The next day, Cindy reached for the phone, dialed the number, and was soon talking with a charming person named Vicky who was the transplant coordinator at Penn State Children's Hospital in Hershey. Vicky provided extensive details about what was involved and some of the risks. Then she promised to send Cindy a packet of information explaining that if the initial blood tests didn't rule her out, she would be asked if she was willing to undergo a full day of testing at Penn State Children's Hospital, an eighty-minute drive away. Finally, Vicky cautioned that there was an 80 percent likelihood that she would not meet the donor requirements.

Cindy decided to take one more step forward. Confiding in no one other than her husband and still unsure about becoming a donor, she continued to feel that exploring the matter until she had all the necessary information was the right thing to do. It wasn't long until she received a notice that her day of testing was scheduled for October 25.

❄

The night before her appointment, Cindy drove to Hershey and stayed at a nearby hotel so she could be at the hospital at the crack of dawn.

Before going to bed, she wanted to be sure that she was doing what God wanted her to do. She prayed for protection for her husband and her children, and she prayed for the Ernst family.

As she thought about Katelynn, Cindy again felt for the parents. Here she was, taking a bold step of faith, and the Ernst family was being kept in the dark. There was no way for them to know what Cindy was doing, for it was against hospital policy to share patient information.

Those parents must be so worried for their little girl, thought Cindy, opening her computer. Locating the family's Facebook page, she clicked the message icon and wrote a short paragraph:

> *I wanted to send you a message to introduce myself since tomorrow I am heading to Hershey Med Center for a full day of tests and meetings to possibly become Katelynn's living donor.*

Alicia and Chris were out shopping when Alicia's phone dinged that she had a message. She clicked the

Facebook notifier, whooped out loud, and then excitedly read the message to Chris. It ended:

I'm Cindy Santos, and I met Katelynn in school. I was a substitute teacher in her class.

Alicia and Chris, though wary of being hopeful, couldn't help themselves. They hugged each other long and hard in the aisle of the store!

At the end of her day of testing, Cindy was told that the results would take about four weeks to evaluate. The hospital would let her know the outcome at the end of November.

❄

Five days after her trip to Hershey, on October 30, Cindy had another Godwink: she had been reassigned to Richmond Elementary School—not as a teacher this time but as a teacher's aide in various classes. She smiled inwardly when she saw that one of the classes in which she was scheduled to spend thirty minutes was kindergarten. And one of the four children she would work with was Katelynn Ernst.

(Wow—more divine alignment of Godwinks!)

As she held up flash cards for her darling little friend, Cindy couldn't help thinking about the Godwinks that were popping up. *Of all the kids in this school, here I am sitting with Katelynn, and she has no clue that just days ago, I went through massive testing to possibly save her life.*

She reminded herself that she had not yet fully come to terms with the what-ifs: *What if they decide that I am qualified—that I'm in the 20 percent chance for candidacy? What should I do? Should I say yes?*

She couldn't help but wonder if the series of Godwinks was God's means of encouraging her. Then, in a moment of sober thought, she asked herself, *Am I really following God's plan—or is this my own plan?*

Cindy's session with Katelynn was suddenly interrupted. Another teacher's aide rushed in and said to Cindy, in a low voice, that she needed to escort Katelynn to the principal's office right away; her mother was there to pick her up. In a whispered aside, the teacher excitedly added, "They're rushing her to Hershey Children's Hospital. They've found a kidney donor for Katelynn!"

Cindy watched the back of her little friend as she was ushered from the classroom. *Well, God, maybe this is a sign. And if You have another way to save this child, hallelujah!*

But as Cindy went on to her other classes, she found herself needing to sweep away the pesky question that kept creeping into her consciousness: *Am I disappointed that the donor isn't me?*

❄

Alicia Ernst received a call from Hershey that they had a deceased donor and the kidney was a match, so she and Katelynn should please get to the hospital as soon as possible! Alicia ran to the car and telephoned Chris as she drove to pick up Katelynn at school. He said he'd leave right away and meet them back at the house.

"Katelynn didn't know what was going on," says Alicia. "After all, she was only five. When I picked her up from school, she seemed so frail. She was always exhausted after the dialysis every night. Still, we needed to get her to the hospital as quickly as possible."

The medical team in Hershey quickly prepped Katelynn, giving Alicia and Chris a few moments to step into the hall, where they could pray. Down the hallway they saw a family gathered, crying together. Alicia and Chris could tell that they were grieving a lost child.

"God, please be with them," prayed Alicia, "and with us."

When Alicia and Chris returned to the room, they were cautiously hopeful that in just minutes Katelynn would be given a new kidney, a new lease on life. As nurses were hooking up Katelynn's IV, the phone rang. It was the operating room. The doctor wanted to speak with both parents.

"I'm sorry," he said. "The kidney from the deceased donor is not functioning properly. We cannot do the transplant."

Their hopes were dashed yet again.

Alicia began to sob, and Chris squeezed his lips together to keep from crying.

"God has a plan," said Alicia, her voice breaking. "I just know He has a plan."

"We have to keep believing that," counseled Chris.

"Let's remember that Katelynn's teacher was tested. Maybe *she's* the one."

In his mind he asked himself, *Do I really believe that? It's such a struggle to believe anymore.*

※

Cindy felt she needed more information. Later that day she decided to check Katelynn's Kidney Journey on Facebook to see if anything was there.

Her heart sank. She read that Katelynn had not received the transplant. She felt so sorry that the Ernst family's hopes had once again been raised and then shattered. Suddenly she felt a little worried. *What if I don't qualify to be her donor? How much can that child—and her parents—bear?*

Even though Cindy was waiting patiently to receive a call from Vicky at Penn State Children's Hospital, she was surprised when the phone rang the day after Thanksgiving. Vicky said excitedly, "You have been approved to be Katelynn's kidney donor!"

Cindy felt a huge rush of emotion. She was glad she was now in a position to say yes—to save Katelynn's life—but face-to-face with the decision, she asked herself, *Will I? Is this the right thing for* my *family?*

Vicky continued speaking about the report. She said that Cindy's daylong testing had turned up something unusual: she had a rare medical disorder called pelvic congestive condition.

"Oh, my," said Cindy. "I've had severe stomach pain on occasion. But the pain would subside, so I've never bothered to get it checked."

"Well," said Vicky, "the doctors evaluating your case called in a specialist, an ob-gyn, to ask if that condition would disqualify you as a donor. They were told that, on the contrary, the removal of one of your kidneys would relieve the pressure on the pelvis and thereby forestall certain surgery for you in the future."

Wow! Another Godwink! Cindy was having a hard time counting all of them.

Do I really need any more divinely aligned nudges before I step out in faith and agree to be Katelynn's donor? Cindy asked herself.

Vicky continued, "This type of surgery is done on Tuesdays, and we can schedule you and Katelynn for December 17. What do you think?"

Cindy hesitated. There was a moment of noticeable dead air. "Well . . . do you think we could try to have it scheduled earlier?" she asked. "That way Katelynn and I could both be home for Christmas."

Vicky agreed to try.

And Cindy realized that she'd just made the commitment.

※

Vicky called back a short while later and asked, "Will December 10 work for you?"

"Yes!" said Cindy.

With only about two weeks to go before the surgery, Cindy still felt a small disconnect because she hadn't yet met Katelynn's parents. Then, six days before the procedure, Cindy was asked to go to the hospital for preadmission testing.

"Katelynn and her parents will be there on the same day for Katelynn's preadmission," said the administrator, "but we don't know what time."

A friend of Cindy's volunteered to drive her to the hospital. The friend's mom lived in Hershey, so while Cindy was doing what she had to do, the friend would visit her mom and then swing back to pick up Cindy.

Alicia and Chris had also been told that Cindy would be on the hospital premises, but it was not known when. "There she is!" said Alicia excitedly, recognizing Cindy from her Facebook photos as Chris drove into the hospital parking lot. "She's standing right there at the curb!"

(More and more divine alignment of Godwinks!)

Chris pulled over. The three jumped out of the car, ran toward Cindy, and introduced themselves. The adults shared a group hug. Then, when Cindy got down to her level, Katelynn's hug was the warmest of all.

It was during that small chat that yet another Godwink was revealed. They discovered that they had also been divinely aligned geographically. Both families live in Blandon, Pennsylvania, and their homes are within walking distance of each other!

❄

On the evening of December 9, Cindy's parents stayed overnight with the boys while Matt and Cindy drove to Hershey. They had made reservations at the same hotel Cindy had stayed at for her day of testing. And that was the setting for one more Godwink—a confirmation that God was right there next to them. When they walked into their room, Cindy realized it was the very room she had stayed in before.

❄

It was still dark when Cindy and Matt arrived at the hospital the next morning. Her prep was scheduled for 6 a.m. They were told that Cindy would go into surgery first and have her kidney removed.

As Cindy lay on the hospital gurney, she began to shiver. It was cool in the room, and she was wearing only a hospital gown. But she knew that her shaking was not because she was cold. Her anxiety was peaking.

"I was so nervous. I had to keep praying, *Please, God! Give me the strength I need.*"

She tried to sort out her feelings. She hadn't been this nervous even when her boys were born! *Why am I so scared now, God?*

She realized that during childbirth she had been concerned only about herself and her baby. But in this situation, so much more was at stake. She began to think of all the risks that Vicky had been required to tell her, as part of the hospital's full disclosure. Those risks were now spelled out in her mind in neon letters. *I'm now taking risks with the mother of my children—and the wife of my husband. My risks also affect the life of a sweet five-year-old girl—and her parents . . . her sisters and her brother.*

Cindy continued to shake. A nurse brought her a warm blanket.

Then Cindy thought about the deacons at her church. The pastor had asked the congregation to pray for her as she approached the big day. One deacon had given Cindy a verse from the Bible, Deuteronomy 31:8, and Cindy had memorized it. Lying on the gurney, she began to recite it:

> *The LORD himself goes before you*
> *and will be with you;*
> *he will never leave you nor forsake you.*
> *Do not be afraid; do not be discouraged.*

Soon a feeling of peace and comfort washed over her, and she stopped shaking.

A short while later she went into surgery to have one of her kidneys removed. Katelynn would follow and receive the gift of life—perhaps more specifically, the gift of a lifetime from a substitute teacher who had been *divinely aligned, Godwink by Godwink*, into her classroom.

Cindy and Katelynn were both released from the hospital in plenty of time to be home with their families for Christmas—and what a joyous Christmas that was!

❋

From that day forward, Cindy Santos has played a large role in Katelynn's Kidney Journey. The two—as well as Alicia and Chris—can see, with great clarity, a trail of amazing Godwinks that divinely aligned their paths for that very purpose.

Cindy and Katelynn see each other occasionally throughout the year. But there are two dates that they never miss celebrating: Katelynn's birthday, August 20, and her "kidney-versary," December 10.

"Everything played out like Cindy was sent from Heaven," says Katelynn's mom. "She's an angel."

"No, I'm not," insists Cindy. "But I do believe I was put into Katelynn's classroom not by coincidence but by divine intervention."

"We feel exactly the same way," says Alicia. "God sent Cindy to us."

"It makes you appreciate life," adds Chris. "This experience has strengthened our faith and brought my wife and me closer together."

Katelynn now leads a normal life. She is active, happy, and healthy. And the screen saver on her phone is a darling picture of Cindy and her together.

REFLECTIONS

Discovering the gift of divinely aligned Godwinks—the invisible threads that connect you to people and circumstances that God wants you to experience—enables you to appreciate just how much God loves you to be so incredibly attached to every aspect of your life, every day of the year.

He had a grand plan for Cindy to meet little Katelynn by assigning her as Katelynn's kindergarten teacher just one time. That was all it took for Him to start weaving the threads of divine alignment to save Katelynn's life.

For I know the plans that I have for you,
declares the LORD, plans for well-being,
and not for calamity . . . to give you a future and a hope.
—JEREMIAH 29:11 (NASB)

27

Renee: Mysterious Memories of Christmas

"Oh, honey, I'll be fine!" said Renee's mother over the phone.

Renee couldn't help fretting about her mother's health issues. Her mom, Darlene, was only sixty-six, yet she worried and called her every day. Whenever possible, Darlene would drive down to Clinton, about an hour and a half from Kansas City, to check up on her.

"I wish you could make it for Christmas, Mom," lamented Renee.

Her mother lived in a small single-story apartment for the handicapped, so it made sense for everyone to gather in the Kansas City area, often at Renee's more spacious home or sometimes at the home of Maegen, Renee's niece. For several years, Darlene's older sister, Betty, had driven the two of them up for Christmas dinner.

"Oh, honey, I wish I could come, but you know what the doctor said: avoid travel. And the weather doesn't look good.

But, honestly, Betty and I will be fine. We'll have a little Christmas spirit right here by ourselves. Don't you worry about it."

When Renee hung up, she was resolved: she told her family that she had a very strong feeling—almost a sense of urgency—that they should all go to Grandma's house this year, perhaps arriving at different times, even on different days, in order to accommodate the space limitations of her small home.

Renee left it to her three grown children and her niece to work out the schedules so everyone could lift Grandma's spirits for Christmas.

Renee and her husband, Jim, arranged to go down on Christmas Day, and over the holidays literally everyone went to Clinton and spent time with Grandma Darlene.

Renee's grandkids conspired together and decided to surprise their great-grandmother with plaster imprints of their hands. It was a very special gift, and she was tickled.

❄

Four weeks later, Renee was awakened by the dreaded sound of the phone ringing in the middle of the night. It was Aunt Betty with sad news.

"Renee, your mom has gone home to be with the Lord." She broke into tears, trying to control her voice.

Renee was shocked. "What? No!"

Even though everyone had known her mother was in poor health, no one had thought it was that serious.

Her aunt went on, "I was sleeping in the spare bedroom and heard her call out my name—'Betty!' I jumped up, got to her bedside—and she was struggling to breathe. Then she was gone."

Renee's own sobs melded with those of her aunt, who continued, "That was the last word she spoke: 'Betty!'" She cried some more.

Renee was crushed. "My mom was my best friend, my rock, and my sounding board."

❄

Three days later, in the evening, the family was invited to gather at the funeral home in Kansas City for a visitation.

Renee was making last-minute arrangements. She telephoned Aunt Betty in the morning to ask her to stop by her mother's apartment to pick up some things before driving up. She asked her to gather whatever photographs she could find so they could be displayed at the visitation and then at the funeral the next day.

"One more thing: the grandkids had their handprints imprinted in plaster as a keepsake for their great-grandmother. They thought that would be a nice remembrance, along with the photos. Could you see if you can find them, please? I don't know where Mom kept them."

It was just after nine when Betty arrived at her sister's home. She wanted to have plenty of time to find everything Renee needed, but she was running a little late and she was feeling out of sorts that morning. It was a cold, bleak day. *Just plain dreary*, she thought.

She pulled up to the apartment, walked to the door, put the key into the lock, and entered the dark and empty home. *On second thought*, she mused, *it doesn't feel dreary, it feels eerie.*

Why it felt that way, she didn't quite know. She'd actually been living in this apartment for the past four months, watching over her sister. But, she rationalized, when a loved one graduates to Heaven, the spaces left behind seem extra empty.

I feel empty myself, she thought.

In Darlene's bedroom she picked up several photos from her sister's dresser and placed them in a tote bag. She looked around but saw no other pictures and no sign of the kids' plaster handprints. She checked the closet. Under the bed. Behind the door.

Leaving the room, she moved on to check the utility closet near the kitchen. She saw the ironing board but no sign of the children's plaster artwork. Now she began to worry that she might disappoint the kids.

She tried to keep herself from crying. *Why shouldn't I cry?* she thought. *My dear sister just died.*

Suddenly she was startled. Sounds were coming from her sister's bedroom. Music! A familiar Christmas hymn, playing faintly.

She took a few tentative steps back toward the bedroom. With all of her senses on alert, she slowly walked toward Darlene's dresser. The music got louder.

There in the jewelry box sat Darlene's pin—the one she had worn every Christmas, shaped like a brass trumpet lying on a green background, with gold flowers and a red ribbon.

"I haven't heard that pin play for years," whispered Betty. "How could that be?"

In an instant she felt a peace flow over her. She knew that God was sending her a very special message directly from Heaven—that her sister was there, with Him, at His side.

When Betty arrived at the funeral home in Kansas City, she apologized profusely to Renee that she'd been unsuccessful in finding the grandchildren's plaster handprints. But she couldn't wait to tell Renee about the special Godwink that she had received: music from Heaven.

Renee was astonished by the story. She, too, knew that the old pin hadn't made a sound in years. There was no reason to doubt her aunt. She just wished she could have heard it, too.

❄

A few weeks later, Renee's unarticulated prayer was answered. She was cleaning out her mother's home, packing things up.

She felt melancholy for her mom. That's when she heard it.

"The sound was coming from the broken pin, just like Aunt Betty described; mimicking a toy whose batteries had long since faded but struggled to play anyway," she said.

Somehow that sound from her mother's special pin, worn every Christmas, brought her a measure of closure. "I'm so glad I got to hear it myself. I looked up and said, 'I love you, too, Mom.'"

She has since kept her mother's favorite Christmas pin on display in her curio cabinet. That way she can have it close to her year-round.

And who knows, maybe it'll mysteriously play its music again one day.

"I hope so," says Renee with a smile.

REFLECTIONS

Some experiences are simply inexplicable.

God has no boundaries, and His presence can be seen and heard in many different ways.

Look how He used a sentimental musical pin, hidden from sight in a dresser, to connect Renee and Betty to their beloved Darlene supernaturally, giving both of them an inexplicable comfort.

God communicates with each of us every day, everywhere, and in everything. We just need to open our spiritual eyes and ears to discover the hidden treasures He has promised us.

Each one is a gift.

> *I will give you hidden treasures,*
> *riches stored in secret places*
> *so that you may know that I am the Lord.*
> —Isaiah 45:3 (NIV)

28

Tom: A Miraculous Christmas

This is a story about an astonishing Godwink—a real-life miracle that happened to a real-life medical doctor who lives today.

To put this story into context, we want to share the answer to the one question we have heard more than any other, in twenty-five years of our study: How do I get more Godwinks?

To anyone paying attention, we say, the answer is very simple: pray more.

That's right. More prayer equals more Godwinks.

If you wish to experience an amazing Godwink, like the one you're about to read, follow Dr. Tom's example, which was supported by his family, friends, and church.

❉

Dr. Tom Renfro lives in the small community of Norton, Virginia, population 4,500. He's a well-respected physician, loved by many.

When his town heard the terrible news that Tom had been diagnosed with mantle cell lymphoma, stage 4—the final stage of the cancer—they were devastated.

The diagnosis was confirmed by the University of Virginia, Dr. Renfro's alma mater, and he was told there was no cure, that this type of lymphoma often marches right through chemotherapy and that bone marrow and stem cell transplants generally fail to cure it.

"Go home and enjoy what time you have left," the doctors there advised.

Tom's oncologist, Dr. Steven Woodley, also leveled with him: "Once you reach this extensive stage of the disease, odds are approaching zero that you'll ever be disease free."

❋

Tom made a decision that might have seemed odd at the time, to videotape his last few months of life. Over the next few weeks, as the cancer progressed, it was painful to see how it ravaged his body.

Above the surface, the videotape revealed baseball-sized tumors popping up all over: on his neck, under his arms, and on his abdomen. Beneath the surface, blood clots were targeting his lungs and heart. He was beginning to suffer from multiorgan failure, malnutrition, and ulcers.

How could his hopeless story ever turn to hope?

Through prayer. The stubborn, nonstop prayers of a believing church!

Tom's congregation refused to give up on him. They loved him and committed to pray for him for twelve hours a day for forty days. Often people prayed throughout the night. When they reached the end of forty days, they started praying another forty days.

It seemed as though the more the congregation prayed, the worse he got. Still, they dug in their heels and prayed even more.

When Tom's kidneys began to fail, doctors knew the end was near. Now their short-range goal was simply to keep him alive until Christmas. Their last-ditch plan was to squeeze out a few more days of life by administering chemotherapy.

Yet before the chemo even began, something miraculous happened. Tom's wife, Sid, said she witnessed the most powerful manifestation of the Holy Spirit she's ever seen: "All of a sudden, the tumors melted away. They were gone! There was no more cancer!"

That was a Christmas miracle like no other!

Tom's army of prayer warriors felt the joy of witnessing the power of their relentless beseeching of the Lord.

Dr. Woodley said, "I felt that Tom was miraculously cured, and through his faith, God worked to preserve his life."

❋

Just two weeks after Christmas, Tom stood in front of his church, tearfully expressing his joy. "I want you to understand that this is a true miracle. This is what you have been praying for! I don't have the words to express what is in my heart, nor what God has done for me, but you are looking at a true miracle of God!"

❋

If Tom hadn't videotaped his journey, most people wouldn't have believed it. But the town of Norton and the surrounding county saw for themselves what can happen when a praying church is faithful to the power of God; their prayers were answered when the almighty God intervened and saved a friend who had been given no hope.

❋

A few months later, Tom and Sid headed to Israel, where he was baptized in the Jordan River. With arms raised in victory, he shouted, through tears of joy, "Glory to God! Glory to God!"

Once again healthy, Dr. Tom is doing today what he does best: being a doctor and helping others get well.

REFLECTIONS

Why does God choose to heal some people but not others?

No one will be able to answer that question with certainty until we sit at His feet and ask Him directly.

We know from the ancient scriptures that persistence of prayer, a firm belief in God, and the expectation that you will receive a successful outcome[1] each plays a role in answered prayer. But why God allows some people and not others to receive a miraculous healing like Dr. Tom Renfro's will remain a mystery. Even the apostle Paul, who had amazing faith, was not healed after he asked God three times.

We can only trust that God is aware of our suffering and that He has a higher purpose for it.

In the meantime, the gift of prayer works. And prayer produces Godwinks.

When I pray, coincidences happen; when I don't, they don't.

—SIR WILLIAM TEMPLE

29

Theresa: The Sweet Smell of Christmas

Theresa Mendelson's small house in Metairie, Louisiana, was gaily decorated for Christmas, accented by the holly tree in the middle of the front lawn.

On Christmas Eve the family gathered at her house, and on Christmas Day they would celebrate at her brother's home.

Over Christmas Eve dinner Theresa comforted a family member who had recently lost her dad. She told the young woman that she could feel her pain; that although she had lost her own mom thirty years earlier, not a day went by that she didn't miss her or think about her.

The young woman said that since her father's passing she had received several Godwinks that had comforted her. Theresa commented that she'd learned from her own experience that Godwinks were common at times of sorrow.

Then, for a moment, she expressed regret that, for some time, she had received no Godwinks relating to her mother. Quickly dismissing her sudden feelings of sadness, she smiled and added, "I know she's always with me in spirit. In fact, this was my mother's home. We decided to move in here a few years after she was gone."

❅

The next day, before driving to her brother's home, as a usual safety measure, Theresa and her husband checked to see that all the Christmas lights were turned off, including the snowman that stood on a side table like a large snow globe.

They had a wonderful Christmas holiday. When they returned home in Metairie, it was after dark. As Theresa went into the house, she was instantly puzzled—the foot-tall snowman was lit up, and the glitter inside was dancing about.

For a few moments she and her husband stood looking at the snowman, trying to retrace their steps.

"I remember turning it off when we went to bed last night," she said. "Besides, I got up in the middle of the night and would have seen it on."

Just then her husband asked, "What's that sweet smell?"

Together they sniffed the air, commenting that it was the aroma of something strong and flowery.

"I don't have any flowers or candles," said Theresa, "so it can't be that."

They walked from room to room to see if the scent was replicated anywhere else in the house. It wasn't.

Suddenly Theresa stopped with a puzzled look on her face. "Can it be?" She sniffed the air again. "It is!" She looked at her husband, who had no clue what she was talking about.

"It's Mother's Estée Lauder perfume. She always wore it."

She explained that her mother always had a big powder puff in a box of Estée Lauder powder in her bathroom, and she had used the perfume every day.

The sweet scent that seemed to replicate Estée Lauder lasted a short while longer. Then it was gone.

Later Theresa reflected, "To get this Godwink at Christmas made it all the more special. It was my Christmas gift from Heaven. It was like she was right here with me—and I'll cherish it forever."

REFLECTIONS

Mothers are comforters.

From toddler to teen, she was there to kiss your boo-boos and wipe away your tears.

Although Theresa's mom had been gone for three decades, Theresa continued to feel her motherly love and comfort.

Imagine her surprise and joy when, within hours of expressing regret to a young woman that she had received no recent Godwinks connecting her to her mother, the room was filled with the gift of her mother's sweet aroma and the snowman snow globe was lit up!

> *Blessed are those who mourn,*
> *for they shall be comforted.*
>
> —Matthew 5:4 (ESV)

30

Robert: A Tapestry of Christmas Love

The storm clouds of winter dissipated over the village where Pastor Robert Nance was preparing for his "grand opening," as he liked to call it. Christmas Eve, just one day away, would inaugurate his assignment to a historic but woefully dilapidated church in upstate New York.

As the heavy doors creaked open, he was anxious to see the newly painted and plastered sanctuary that he and a group of volunteers had completed the evening before, just ahead of the storm.

He stood in the entryway, not in awe but in shock. During the night a leak in the roof had ripped a gaping hole in the wall right behind the pulpit!

264 Godwink Christmas Stories

Oh, no! Now what am I going to do? he asked himself, shaking his head in dismay.

He quickly calculated that there was no way he could round up church volunteers or hire anyone to repair the damage by the next afternoon.

He was crestfallen. For the past two weeks he'd been going door to door, throughout the neighborhood, telling people about the Christmas Eve festivities, inviting them to come to the rejuvenated church, telling them to bring their children, friends, and family.

Now, he thought to himself, nearly tearing up, *I'm letting everyone down. The only thing they'll be staring at, all during the service, is that ugly hole in the wall!*

"Lord, I need a miracle!" he declared aloud, lifting his eyes upward as he turned, and he walked dejectedly toward his study in the back of the church.

He passed through an anteroom, stepping sideways to get around an annoying pile of unsold items from the holiday bazaar, to which someone had attached a handwritten note: "Trash."

He headed toward his study, stopped, and backed up to look at something that caught his eye. He lifted the edges of what appeared to be a huge tablecloth. It was actually an old tapestry, once beautiful and finely woven. Now it was well worn and oversized for any home.

No wonder it didn't sell, he thought.

Then an idea struck him: *Wait. This tapestry could be just the thing I need!*

He pulled a tall ladder out of the back room, lugged it into the sanctuary, and, with a hammer and a few nails, completed his task.

It was past sunset when Pastor Nance left his study and began to exit the church. He turned to take one last look back into the sanctuary before shutting off the lights. With a self-satisfied smile, he gazed upon the "miracle" that God had delivered to him. The old tapestry, nailed to the wall, completely masked the nasty hole.

❈

The pastor had almost reached his car when he realized that he'd absentmindedly left the keys on his desk. Returning to the church, he passed the bus stop, where he spotted a small woman huddled in the cold.

"Hello? How long have you been waiting?" he asked.

Her dark eyes looked at him with uncertainty. She shivered, and her voice was weak as she slowly spoke in accented English: "One hour."

"Come inside and get warm while I get my keys. I can drive you home," he offered.

When Pastor Nance returned from his study, he didn't see the old woman. Then he found her standing behind the pulpit and examining the tapestry in the dim light of the church. Her wrinkled fingers stroked it fondly.

"Dis is mine," she whispered.

"Yours?"

"Yes. Those are my initials," she said, pointing to the corner of the tapestry.

Responding to the confused look on his face, she continued, "In Austria we had a big table. I wove this with my own hands. In the war I lost my home . . . I was separated from my husband"—her voice trailed off as tears glistened in her eyes—"and never saw him again."

In disbelief the pastor stammered, "Y-Y-You . . . must take this with you." He reached for the tapestry.

"No," she forbade him, raising her hand to halt him. "You keep it here. I have no place for it."

It was a quiet ride through the darkened streets. The pastor was nearly speechless as he said good-bye. "I'm going to pray for you," he told her, helping her from the car.

"Thank you," she replied with a slight smile.

He watched her lonely form disappear into her modest dwelling.

On the drive home, Pastor Nance did indeed pray for her. He asked God to bless that dear woman. "Please, God, bless her this Christmas in a manner that she could never have imagined."

Then, as he drove, he pondered the powerful significance of what he had witnessed. *What are the odds that this woman, at a lonely bus stop, would somehow be connected to a tapestry, left for trash, that he had just hung inside the old church to solve a big problem?*

And what an incredible Godwink it was to occur at such

a critical turning point in his own life—the commencement of his new ministry. It was mind-boggling!

"God, You are amazing," he whispered.

✳

Christmas Eve arrived in the hustle and bustle of holiday excitement. Children costumed as small sheep and shepherds scurried to their rehearsed places as a miniature Mary gently cradled a baby doll. Candlelight flickered across Rubenesque faces, and the old church came alive with joyful caroling. As was the tradition, everyone sang "Silent Night" as the final Christmas carol.

Pastor Nance swelled with satisfaction. His "grand opening" had been a success.

At the end of the evening, when the last hand was shaken and the last Merry Christmas wished, he felt a wonderful sense of peace. With everyone gone, he turned to look, just one more time, at the majestic old tapestry hanging in the dim light—the "miracle" that had been delivered to him and that now seemed to be at home behind the pulpit. *Perhaps we should keep it there*, he mused.

But something—a ghostly figure near the tapestry—caused his eyes to narrow.

"Hello?" he asked into the dim light.

No answer.

"Hello?" he repeated, hesitantly stepping closer.

No answer.

"Oh . . ." He sighed. "It's you, Hans." He was relieved that it was only the church custodian.

Hans was staring at the tapestry.

"Is everything all right, Hans?"

"Dis is mine," he answered tentatively, with a Viennese inflection.

"I beg your pardon?"

"Dis is mine. My wife made dis for our home in Austria. Those are her initials. It was with our belongings . . . in the war . . . when we lost each other."

His eyes moistened.

Pastor Nance felt his pulse quickening, his heart beating faster. He couldn't believe that, like a startled spectator, he was witnessing an even *bigger* Christmas miracle: a God-wink beyond dimension and comprehension! He became nearly speechless.

The tapestry was not just the solution for a damaged church wall. It was a tool of the Almighty; a Godwink Link that God was using—the way He was using the pastor himself—to connect two lost souls, from long ago, in a faraway land.

"Hans, would you come with me, please?" asked Pastor Nance. "I need to drive you somewhere. I promise you, this will be the best Christmas gift you've ever received."

❄

It is hard to imagine the joy that bubbled over inside of Pastor Nance—a peace that was tucked into his heart for the rest of his days on Earth—every time he relived that moment in his memory. He stood next to the bewildered Hans, at the door of a strange house, waiting for the door to open and to witness the joy in those two faces— Hans and his long-lost love—ignited by the light of God's love.

Pastor Nance was forever blessed—*richly* blessed—to have been an unwitting messenger, a Godwink Link, in the lives of those two forlorn people.

It was *his* best Christmas ever![1]

REFLECTIONS

Godwinks are ubiquitously woven into the fabric of our lives and are often interlaced by unexpected emissaries of joy—Godwink Links.

Think back to when you played "connect the dots" in a picture book as a kid. After a while a picture of what you were intended to discover began to emerge.

Similarly, God nudges us to connect with people He wants us to meet along our pathways in life. Sometimes you will unknowingly impart something to them that will change their lives, answering their prayers.

On other occasions God intends for you to deliver a message to someone—about a job opportunity, for instance, or even to connect them to a love in their life, as Pastor Nance did for Hans and his long-lost wife.

In each case, you have been a divine connector. God has honored you with the gift of being His Godwink Link.

31

Alice and Jack's Remedy for Love: Let Go

"If you want me to be married, Lord, *you* pick him out. So far my choices stink." Alice was gazing skyward with a look of finality on her face.

With that, she dusted her hands up and down and surrendered the whole matter to God.

Failed relationships were only one of the things bothering her. The latest doctor's report on the condition of her multiple sclerosis was also less than encouraging.

Throwing herself into her job and her part-time studies for a master's degree seemed to be the best antidote.

Not long after Alice let the matter of marriage drift from her mind, she succumbed to her sister's urgings to attend a social event. "It'll do you some good just to get out," goaded her sister.

The event was pretty boring. Alice decided to leave early. As she stepped in front of a man near the exit, her eyes connected with his.

"They were the most beautiful golden-brown eyes I'd ever seen," sighs Alice.

The man introduced himself. His name was Jack. "I think we shook hands for about three minutes," she now remembers with a smile.

They began talking. They talked and talked and talked. After nearly three hours—like Cinderella suddenly looking at her watch—Alice exclaimed: "Ohmygosh . . . I've got to go. I have to study for a test. And I'm going to my cousin's wedding this weekend down in Victoria, Texas, and I'm not ready."

"I'm *also* going to a wedding this weekend in Victoria," said Jack curiously. "*My* cousin's marrying a doctor."

"My cousin *is* a doctor!" shouted Alice.

❄

Two people who had just met, each going to a cousin's wedding eight hours away—the *same* wedding. What are the odds of that?

Moreover—what do you *do* about it?

Save on gas.

They drove the five hundred miles to Victoria together, and there wasn't a moment of dead air—not a single loss for words.

At the wedding reception, Alice and Jack danced, again and again. "My feet hardly touched the floor," she remembers dreamily.

And when he kissed her good night, she said, "It made my toes curl."

The next morning Alice had breakfast with her favorite uncle, Charlie, and couldn't wait to tell him what was on her mind.

"I met the man I'm going to marry," she told Uncle Charlie.

"Does he know it?"

"No. But he's the one. His name is Jack Totah."

"Jack Totah? I wonder if he's related to Nabe Totah," Uncle Charlie said.

Just then, Jack entered the room and joined them. "Yes— he's my uncle out in California," he said.

"You won't believe this," said Uncle Charlie, slowly shaking his head, "but fifty years ago I was on a boat coming to America, filled with uncertainty. I worried what would happen when I landed in this strange new land. Then I met a young man who felt the same as me: Nabe Totah. We became the closest of friends, all across the ocean. When we got to customs, we were separated, and I never saw my buddy Nabe again. I always wondered what happened to him . . ."

As they listened, Alice and Jack looked at each other in disbelief.

This was just another in a powerful combination of Godwinks that seemed to be sending them a confirming message that they were meant for each other.

One other matter did weigh on Alice's mind when she returned home, however. She worried that perhaps when Jack learned about her multiple sclerosis, his feelings for her might change.

"Maybe you shouldn't tell him," counseled one friend.

"No; I have to," said Alice.

When she mustered the courage to tell him, Jack looked at her—then looked down. A moment later he lifted his head to look her in the eyes. "I'm so sorry. What can I do to help you?" he asked.

Jack's response was more than she could have hoped for.

❄

A year later, there was another wonderful wedding.

Alice and Jack's.

One of the most treasured snapshots in Alice's memory bank was when Jack lifted her veil to kiss her. He whispered, "I'll love you forever."

Her heart melted all over again.

Another cherished picture was seeing Uncle Charlie and Uncle Nabe, toasting the bride and groom, standing side by side, reunited after fifty years.

"I found my true soul mate, and Uncle Charlie found his friend," said Alice. "Thank God. I mean, *really* thank God!"

❄

It all began when she surrendered.

It is indeed amazing what happens when we "let go"

in the pursuit of a perfect mate. When we have the courage to do that, we're generally surprised with the results—sometimes guiding us to outcomes that we could never have imagined for ourselves.

Today, four years after I first wrote about Alice and Jack, they continue to grow their love for each other, with God, and with life. And add to that a little boy, Jacob.

Alice struggles with the debilitating effects of multiple sclerosis, and has accepted the concept that the blessing of having one child can be "just enough."

Alice and Jack miss Uncle Nabe—who passed away—but see Uncle Charlie with some frequency, when he isn't fishing.

CONCLUSION

odwink Christmas Stories has sought to show that every **Godwink is a gift,** a beautifully wrapped package left on your doorstep, just for you. Our aim is to inspire you to open the door and open your gift.

Here are some of the memorable "takeaways," the God-wink gifts you've read about in this book.

- Sandy learned that giving just four stamps to an older couple was a huge Godwink for them. **The smallest gift—kindness**—is sometimes the most precious. (Story 1)
- Through a stranger, God showed Jonna that He hadn't forgotten about the desire in her heart—dormant since she was a little girl—to have a recording of "Orange Blossom Special" personally autographed by her heroine. With His **gift of grace** God won't forget your heart desires either. (Story 2)

- Carla's most treasured Christmas started out to be her loneliest—but she learned that the **gift of sharing**, given to her by her friend's family, lasts a lifetime. (Story 3)
- "Godwink," a new word in the language, explains the amazing circumstances through which God brings you the **gift of hope**. (Story 4)
- Gerry tried prayer for the first time and discovered that God was listening. That amazing Godwink delivered him the **gift of a second chance**. And God will do the same for you. (Story 7)
- It was during the Christmas season that Roma visited a children's hospital to spread cheer. But her bonus was a greater clarity about her job for God and the **gift of purpose**. (Story 9)
- In the midst of Candy's holiday hustle-bustle, God showed up with a perfect **gift of encouragement**. And, through a Godwink, He opened the door for her to fulfill her dream to become a writer. (Story 11)
- In restoring the church services in the Capitol Building for the first time in 144 years, Dan discovered that **faith is a gift** from God. Like Dan, you can't see around all the bends in your road, but God can. (Story 12)
- Louise's answer to prayer was totally unexpected as God did something extraordinary, bringing her the **gift of friendship** from a little furry creature she had always longed for. (Story 13)

- Toni discovered that having **the faith of a child is a gift**. Knowing that God places no limits on what you can pray for gave her complete faith that her husband would be healed. Moreover, it would be confirmed with the first snowfall in 109 years. (Story 17)

- Greg's sweet story about his wife, Andrea, who had passed away years before, confirms that Godwinks provide **gifts of memory**—treasures we keep in our hearts forever. (Story 22)

- Ted's story about hearing Kathy's mysterious picture-frame voice teaches us that **God's omnipresence is a gift**. Even when we are not speaking directly to Him, God hears our unarticulated prayers. (Story 23)

- The **gift of the divine alignment of Godwinks** causes us to be at the right place at the right time for God's will to be done. That was shown by Cindy, who was Katelynn's classroom teacher for just one day. But that was enough to save the child's life. (Story 26)

- Dr. Tom's astonishing Christmas miracle affirms that the **gift of prayer** works. Amazingly! And that more prayer produces more Godwinks. (Story 28)

- Pastor Nance was **gifted** the honor to be **a Godwink Link**, God's emissary to connect the lady at the bus stop and church custodian Hans to deliver **God's Christmas gift of Love** to a long-lost couple. (Story 30)

This treasure trove of Christmas Godwinks demonstrates that God is ever present in everything you do and everything around you.

When you develop the ability to see the Godwinks that are unfolding in your life, your entire existence becomes infinitely richer, happier, and more certain.

When you discover that your Creator wants to hear from you—actually wants you to reach out to Him daily, the way you would with a loving parent or grandparent—He will communicate back to you more often and in ways that only He can, through Godwinks.

You'll find that the more you acknowledge God as the source of your Godwinks, the more you will see them. You'll come to the realization that having the ability to see Godwinks is like discovering a pathway to certainty or a steady handrail on a wobbly staircase.

We send you Christmas wishes for joyful and abundant Godwinks!

—SQuire and Louise

NOTES

INTRODUCTION
1 Luke 17:6.

CHAPTER 3: CARLA: A LOST CHRISTMAS—FOUND
1 Joe Raposo and Jon Stone, "One of These Things,"
  Sesame Street Original Cast Record, Vol. 1, lyrics © EMI
  Music Publishing, released January 1, 1970.

CHAPTER 4: SQUIRE: THE BIRTH OF GODWINKS
ON CHRISTMAS EVE
1 Henry J. Devries, *Marketing with a Book: The Science of
  Attracting High-Paying Clients for Consultants and Coaches*
  (Oceanside, CA: Indie Books International, 2015), chap. 2.

CHAPTER 9: ROMA: THE JOB OF A CHRISTMAS ANGEL
1 Roma Downey, *Box of Butterflies: Discovering the Unex-*

pected Blessings All Around (Nashville: Howard Books, 2018), 75; and interviews with the author.
2 Ibid., 77.

CHAPTER 14: YVONNE, PART I: THE SPIRIT
OF CHRISTMAS EVERY DAY
1 Yvonne T. Streit with Jana Mullins, *Everybody's Got a Seed to Sow: The Brookwood Story* (Houston: Bright Sky Press, 2016), 70.
2 Ibid., 75.

CHAPTER 15: YVONNE, PART II: THE REST
OF THE SURPRISING STORY
1 Yvonne T. Streit with Jana Mullins, *Everybody's Got a Seed to Sow: The Brookwood Story* (Houston: Bright Sky Press, 2016), 64–66.

CHAPTER 17: TONI AND DAVID: AN AMAZING
CHRISTMAS MIRACLE
1 "Ejection Fraction," Cleveland Clinic, http://my .clevelandclinic.org/heart/disorders/heartfailure /ejectionfraction.aspx.
2 Baylor Heart Clinic, Echocardiography Report, August 25, 2004, David Espinoza, patient, Guillermo Torre, M.D.
3 *The Monitor*, McAllen, Texas, December 30, 2004.

4 Baylor Heart Clinic, Echocardiography Report, January 24, 2005, David Espinoza, patient, Guillermo Torre, M.D.

CHAPTER 18: RHONDA: HOW CHAD CAME HOME
FOR CHRISTMAS
1 Lee Strobel, *The Case for a Creator: A Journalist Investigates Scientific Evidence That Points Toward God* (Grand Rapids, MI: Zondervan, 2004), 283.

CHAPTER 19: MOLLY: JESUS TOOK THE WHEEL?
1 Hillary Lee Lindsey, Brett James, and Gordon Francis Sampson, "Jesus, Take the Wheel," http://www.songlyrics .com/carrie-underwood/jesus-take-the-wheel-lyrics.

CHAPTER 20: CATHY: CHRISTMAS COOKIES
WITH HEAVENLY DELIVERY
1 Bob Rivers, "Twelve Pains of Christmas," http://www .lyricsfreak.com/b/bob+rivers/12+pains+of+christmas _20149728.html.

CHAPTER 24: BROOKE AND LUKE: EXPECTING
A WONDERFUL LIFE
1 "It's a Wonderful Life," Filmsite Movie Review, http://www.filmsite.org/itsa.html.
2 "What Movie Has Been Aired on TV the Most Times

in History?," comment by Mark Hughes, January 12, 2014, https://www.quora.com/What-movie-has-been -aired-on-TV-the-most-times-in-history.

CHAPTER 28: TOM: A MIRACULOUS CHRISTMAS
1 Matthew 21:22 (KJV).

CHAPTER 30: ROBERT: A TAPESTRY OF CHRISTMAS LOVE
1 There have been other versions of this story by un-known authors on the Internet. The authors based this story on the first known published version in *Reader's Digest*, in 1954.

CLASSIC GODWINK STORIES

"Jonna: The Extraordinary Gift" was previously published as "The 45RPM" in *Godwink Stories* (2012).

"Paula and Gery: A Charlotte Inn Christmas" was previously published as "Paula and Gary [sic]" in *When God Winks on Love* (2004).

"Roma: The Job of a Christmas Angel" was previously published as "My Purpose for God" in *Godwink Stories* (2012).

"Toni and David: An Amazing Christmas Miracle" was previously published as "Toni and David" in *Godwinks and Divine Alignment* (2012).

"Clair: A Picture-Perfect Christmas" was previously published as "Clair Miller's Unbelievably, Unexpected Godwinks" in *When God Winks on Love* (2004).

"Ted: Turning Christmas Blues into Joy" was previously published as "Ted Harris's Christmas Blues Turn to Joy" in *The Godwink Effect* (2017).

"Cindy and Katelynn: An Unforgettable Christmas Wink" was previously published as "Cindy and Katelynn: A Divinely Aligned Wink of Life" in *The Godwink Effect* (2017).

"Tom: A Miraculous Christmas" was previously published as "Tom Renfro: The Awesome Power of a Praying Church" in *The 40 Day Prayer Challenge* (2016).

"Robert: A Tapestry of Christmas Love" was previously published as "The Holiday Tapestry" in *When God Winks on Love* (2004)

SCRIPTURE REFERENCES

MIRACLES OF CHRISTMAS

16 ALL NEW ORIGINAL HOLIDAY MOVIE PREMIERES INCLUDING THE SEQUEL TO *A GODWINK CHRISTMAS*

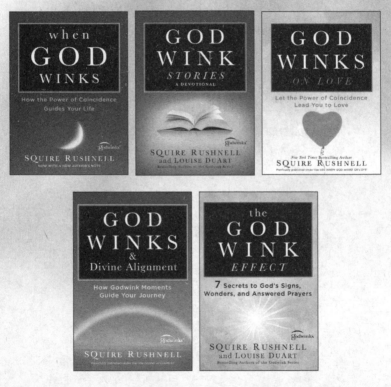